Stoicism - Thinking Like Zeno

The ancient Greek wisdom that is still a sound guide for living life today

A reappraisal in its third millennium, taking into account the ongoing development of the understanding of Nature through the ever-changing modern sciences

by Nigel Glassborow

Sept 2020
Revised September 2021
Revised October 2021

Paperback published and printed 2021 by Moorleys, 23 Park Road, Ilkeston, DE7 5DA
https://www.moorleys.co.uk/

For permissions contact thestoa@hotmail.co.uk

British Library Cataloguing in Publication Data.
A catalogue record for this book is available
from the British Library

ISBN 978 0 86071 872 7

Anyone with a mental illness should seek professional medical help.

While classical Stoicism, and this book, talks of issues regards maintaining 'a sound mind' and aspects of dealing with, avoiding or getting over depression and the like, it is not a therapy, albeit that in many respects Cognitive Behavioural Therapy (CBT) and other similar talking therapies work with similar concepts that Stoicism uses in its mind training.

Classic Stoicism is a life philosophy and belief system where the term philosophy refers to the ancient Greek intent of the word – a love of wisdom.

A Commissioned Publication Printed by

MOORLEYS
Print, Design & Publishing
info@moorleys.co.uk • www.moorleys.co.uk

The views, thoughts, and opinions expressed in this book belong solely to the author, and do not necessarily reflect the views of the publisher or any of its associates.

Index

Page

i   Outline

vi   Introduction

1   1. Just who is this guy called Zeno

7   2. Thinking Like Zeno

20   3. Against overly intellectualising the simplicity of the Stoic rationale

23   4. Stoic understanding and understanding Stoicism

33   5. In Support of Zeno's Metaphysics

67   6. How Zeno's Stoicism is still relevant today

79   7. Control, Determinism and Providence according to the Stoic rationale

89   8. The Stoic s need for a sound mind

97   9.   On Emotional Stability and Attachment

100 10. The Stoic rationale and 'Emotions' in today's world

110 11. The rationale of the Stoic training

122 12. Hierocles Concentric Circles and Caring for Mother Earth

125 13. Taking the Blindfold off the Judge

146 14. Aretê, Character and the Good

149 15. Thinking like a Stoic

157 16. Effective Worrying

161 17. Looking at Mr or Mrs Perfect

164 18. Reading the ancient Stoic texts

175 19. Socrates' 'Divine Something'

182 20. On Fate, Foreknowledge and the Divination

186 21. Restating Stoicism – not reinventing it

190 22. Other Views and Readings

194 23. Two Schools of Stoicism in the 21st Century

199 24. A Stoic Prayer

200 25. Talking with the Cosmos

207 26. On Telepathy and the Quiet Mind

209 **Without the Divine, there is no Stoicism** – a published essay

****

Outline

'Stoicism, a school of thought that flourished in Greek and Roman antiquity, was one of the loftiest and most sublime philosophies in the record of Western civilization. In urging participation in the affairs of man, Stoics have always believed that the goal of all inquiry is to provide man with a mode of conduct characterised by tranquillity of mind and certainty of moral worth.'

'Philosophical Schools & Doctrines - Stoicism', Macropaedia commentary by Jason L Saunders – Encyclopædia Britannica. © 2004 with permission

To some degree, when it comes to living as a Stoic, Stoicism's history and its personalities are an irrelevance. What is important is its simple and unadorned beliefs, in that these beliefs can offer a sound foundation for living a contented and productive life.

All of its beliefs are interlinked and form a sphere of understanding as to the character of things, an understanding that guides the Stoic's approach to their journey through life. This understanding is a combination of an understanding as to the nature of the Universe, the wisdom that has been passed down through the ages and what we may reasonably believe these understandings support when it comes to knowing how to live life. The Stoic faith is supportable by a reasoning that is based on the observation of the nature of the Universe, even taking into account the advances in knowledge since Zeno first collated its foundational principles over two millennia ago.

Stoic wisdom tells us that the whole of the physical Universe is the body of God; that the consciousness that is God permeates the whole of the Universe; and so God, being a single consciousness, manifests and animates the whole of the Universe.

Constantly think of the universe as one living creature, embracing one being and soul; how all is absorbed into the one consciousness of this living creature; how it compasses all things with a single purpose, and how all things work together to cause all that comes to pass, and their wonderful web and texture.
Marcus Aurelius IV.40

'There are two general principles in the universe, the active and the passive. That the passive is matter, an existence without any distinctive quality. That the active is the reason which exists in the passive, that is to say God. For that he being eternal, and existing throughout all matter, makes everything.'
Diogenes Laertius LXVIII

'To live according to virtue is the same thing as living according to one's experience of those things which happen by nature; .... Our individual natures are all parts of universal nature, and that means corresponding to one's own nature and to universal nature; doing none of those things which the common law of mankind is in the habit of forbidding, and that common law is identical with that right reason that pervades everything, being the same with God, who is the regulator and chief manager of all existing things.'
Diogenes Laertius LIII

'The universal nature' is seen as being one and the same as that which we refer to as God, in that the 'active principle' (being 'the right reason that pervades everything') and God are, in Stoicism, both seen as being 'the regulator and chief manager of all existing things'.

Stoicism tells us that, being part of the Universe, we are each created out of the body and mind of God and so ought to live with such knowledge as one of our guiding principles.

Meanwhile, I follow the guidance of Nature – a doctrine upon which all Stoics are agreed. Not to stray from Nature and to mould ourselves according to her law and pattern – this is true wisdom.
Seneca On the Happy Life iii

'The chief good is confessedly to live according to Nature; which is to live according to virtue, for Nature leads us to this point.'
Diogenes Laertius LIII

Being manifested out of the body and soul of God, we have access to a part of the spectrum that is the Consciousness that permeates the whole Universe, and so we take part in determining, to a limited extent, the flow of change that is Existence.

Thus, Stoics believe that God has set the limits of our state-of-being through the laws of Nature, but in the process has given us an element of free-will, and at the same time offers guidance as to how we ought to make use of our free-will for the good of the play of life, such guidance mostly being accessed through awareness of the realities of life and through the application of wisdom.

At the same time, in keeping with Socrates' description of his 'daemon', it is to be seen that at times we can have access to a wider range of 'information' than we normally do as individuals.

"You have often times and in many places heard me give – that there comes to me a something divine and spiritual, which Meletus indeed, by way of a joke, has included in his

indictment; and this is a voice which since childhood has frequently come to me, and which makes itself heard only to turn me back from what I am about to do, but never to impel me forward."
Socrates' Apology

We can discover much of the guidance for living life for ourselves by looking to the wisdom that has stood the test of time, as well as to the character of all about us, in that this helps to inform us as to the nature of the Existence we have been born into – and it is a Stoic principle that knowledge as to the nature of life will help us to learn how to live life. However, as is exampled by Socrates' experience, Stoicism accepts that God will also offer us access to a wider spectrum of awareness through such manifestations as Socrates' daemon.

'God is near you, he is with you, he is within you… A holy spirit indwells within us. One who marks our good deeds and our bad deeds, and is our guardian. Indeed, no man can be good without the help of God. … He it is that gives noble and upright counsel.'
Seneca XLI. On the God Within Us

Based on this background belief, in keeping with all true beliefs, Stoicism guides us to act out our individual lives in the manner that is to be recognised as that of a person of good character who acts with good intent.

To this end, Stoicism guides us to apply reason and wisdom to all that we do. In that wisdom is the good use of knowledge, we need to be able to see the realities of life as best we can and in a manner that offers a clarity of understanding as to how we ought to harmonise with all that is about us.

v

So that we can make good choices in life, Stoicism teaches us to ensure that we look to the reality of any given situation, free from any false perceptions that may be caused by hasty and unexamined first impressions, habituated counterproductive opinions and untamed feelings, instincts and emotions.

Stoicism accepts that many thoughts may enter our minds, but what matters is the choices we make regards which thoughts we follow up on and which we reject. The person who has developed a good character will be the person who chooses to act on those thoughts and perceptions that serve the greater good.

"Mankind have been created for the sake of one another."
Marcus Aurelius VIII.59

"The wise [are] born to be of help to all and to serve the common good."
Seneca On Mercy Iiii

Stoicism teaches us that we can be ready to adapt to circumstance, while having a firm foundation for our worldview – a foundation that will help us through both the good and the not so good times whereby we will remain true to our ethos while trying to serve all around us as best we can.

Introduction

The original extant writings of Stoicism have, for over two millennia, gone through a number of translations and interpretations that aim to try to offer as accurate an understanding of the original writings as possible. However, a key aspect of traditional classic Stoicism is its reliance on what is called 'natural philosophy.' That is, Stoicism states that we can only really learn how to live by studying the world about us – the inquiry into the physical nature of life. And of course, since its inception, and especially over the last 150 years, our understanding of the physical nature of life has improved. So, to be true to Stoicism there is a need to consider its principles against the present state of knowledge so as to come up with new explanations and wording that such inquiries may make necessary in order to keep Stoicism relevant for today.

Professor Gilbert Murray [1866 – 1957] (described as an outstanding scholar of the language and culture of Ancient Greece, and considered as being perhaps the leading authority in the first half of the twentieth century on such matters), gave a lecture at the South Place Institute on the 16th of March 1915 entitled 'The Stoic Philosophy'.

In it he tells us that Stoicism is both a religion and a philosophy. Of course, we are looking at the word 'religion' as referring to Stoicism involving a degree of faith, but not as a faith with the ritual and hierarchy that is to be found in most world religions. Stoicism is not a 'revealed faith' but rather a reasoning that leads to an understanding that involves a framework of belief. And when it comes to the word 'philosophy' we are not looking at a branch of academic philosophy, but back to the original intent of the word philosophy as 'the love of wisdom' - that being its direct translation from the Greek.

When it comes to 'rationality' in this respect, we can borrow from Wikipedia:

"Rationality is the quality or state of being rational – that is, being based on or agreeable to reason. Rationality implies the conformity of one's beliefs with one's reasons to believe, and of one's actions with one's reasons for action.

To determine what behaviour is the most rational, one needs to make several key assumptions, …… When the goal or problem involves making a decision, rationality factors in all information that is available (e.g., complete or incomplete knowledge). Collectively, the formulation and background assumptions are the model within which rationality applies. Rationality is relative: if one accepts a model in which benefitting oneself is optimal, then rationality is equated with behaviour that is self-interested to the point of being selfish; whereas if one accepts a model in which benefiting the group is optimal, then purely selfish behaviour is deemed irrational. It is thus meaningless to assert rationality without also specifying the background model assumptions describing how the problem is framed and formulated."

[https://en.wikipedia.org/wiki/Rationality as at 20th September 2019]

So we have need for a set of "formulation and background assumptions" that define the rationale that is Stoicism – and we have these in what are called the Stoic 'principles'.

So Stoicism insists that the knowledge as to how to live needs to be supportable by reason, reason that is based on what we may logically deduce from our experience of the existence into which we have been born – and in order to explain all of this, we need to have "the background model assumptions describing how the problem is framed and formulated".

To understand the Stoic rationale we need to have, as a starting point, the Stoic "background model assumptions" that tells us how we can know 'what is', what such logically informs us about how best to cope with life, and what such informs us about how to best live our lives.

Stoicism offers a certainty and a confidence regards how to live life through its insistence that the rationale of the Stoic system requires that all choices with regard to how to live have to be based in a reasoning that is rooted in a logical understanding of the nature of the existence in which we find ourselves.

The Stoics divide reason according to philosophy, into three parts; and say that one part relates to natural philosophy, one to ethics, and one to logic. And Zeno, the Cittiaean, was the first who made this division, in his treatise on Reason.
Diogenes Laertius, XXXVIII.

As with any structure that stands on three pillars, the Stoic understanding of natural philosophy, ethics and logic is that all three are equally necessary to support the Stoic reasoning in that they may be seen to be differing aspects of what is effectively the singular rationale that is behind the teaching that is Stoicism. And, when talking of 'natural philosophy,' Stoicism is talking of the actual physical nature of anything and everything that is part of the Cosmos, albeit as seen from the specifically Stoic materialistic viewpoint.

All of which is why Stoicism works best as a whole, whereby the three pillars and the various foundational principles form the basis of its rationality and its guidance "to live in accord with Nature." It is claimed that the aim to "live in accord with Nature" is the one thing that defines what it is to be a follower of Stoicism in that it is the one thing on which every 'Stoic' is agreed.

Meanwhile, I follow the guidance of Nature – a doctrine upon which all Stoics are agreed. Not to stray from Nature and to

mould ourselves according to her law and pattern – this is true wisdom.
Seneca On the Happy Life iii

"To live in accord with Nature" means that Stoicism is ultimately a personal construct, for the individual's own nature is part of the overall Nature that is the Cosmos. To the considerations that are the core of the Stoic system on how to live life, each person has need to add in the consideration as to what their own individual nature brings to the table and as to what of their character they have need to develop or to mitigate so as to best harmonise with all that is around them in a manner that will be of the greatest benefit to the whole.

Stoicism is an outward looking positive view of life, whereby any self-improvement in our skill at living life is aimed at how we may best serve the 'play of life' in which each of us is but one actor. Stoicism looks for selfless commitment to fulfilling all of our roles in life as best we can and in as appropriate a manner as is to be expected in any given situation. Stoicism is about putting all of the theory into practice – in the end it is actions rather than words that count, as is to be expected from a teaching that is so heavily influenced by the nature of its version of materialism.

In studying or practicing Stoicism, it is well to remember that, in keeping with some of the fundamental Stoic principles, the three Stoics of old from whom we have the most extant writings, Seneca, Epictetus and Marcus Aurelius, were all theists - a factor that was fundamental to their opining and their ethics, the very ethics that so many people today want to emulate.

In keeping with Professor Murray's view and that of the eminent professorial experts in the history of Stoicism up to the present day, Stoicism as a whole presents an unashamedly rationalised pantheistic stance as part of its "formulation and background assumptions" that is part of its absolute materialism that is a core of the Stoic system; in that Stoicism sees the Cosmos as being a singular living state where 'the Consciousness' that is the 'agency' that permeates the whole Cosmos is God, in that it is 'the universal governor and organiser of all things', albeit that the Stoic 'principles' do not set 'God,' as the agency of the whole Cosmos, as being totally dictatorial. Stoicism does not see the Cosmos as only governing in a top-down fashion, but rather it operates as the coordinator, coordinating the input of all of its individualised parts, including us as individuals.

There are two consequences of the rationale behind the Stoic version of pantheism. One is that God is, moment by moment, seen as coordinating the flow of change that is existence in a providential way – that is, the flow of change that is Existence happens as a result of reasoned intent and the laws of Nature. (This is the Stoic version of determinism). The second consequence is that we as individuals are seen to be part of the living Cosmos and so we share in determining the progress of the flow of existence within our sphere of influence, and as such, Stoicism guides us to exercise any influence we may be able to exert in a providential manner – that is, with forethought and with the aim of such being for the good of the whole.

A few Stoic students of old may have taken an atheistic stance, but their ideas did not stand the test of time. The consensus regards the Stoicism that has come down to us in the modern world is that it involves a form of pantheism that is an integral part of the Stoic world view.

'We do not need to uplift our hands towards heaven… as if in this way our prayers were more likely to be heard. God is near you, he is with you, he is within you… A holy spirit indwells within us. One who marks our good deeds and our bad deeds, and is our guardian. Indeed, no man can be good

without the help of God. ... He it is that gives noble and upright counsel.'
Seneca XLI. On the God Within Us

I.III. 'If a man could only subscribe heart and soul, as he ought, to the doctrine, that we are all primarily begotten of God, ... I think that he will entertain no ignoble or mean thought about himself.'
I.IV. 'If what is said by the philosophers regarding the kinship of God and men be true, what other course remains for men but that which Socrates took when asked to what country he belonged, never to say "I am an Athenian," or "I am a Corinthian," but "I am a citizen of the universe"?'
IV.VII. 'For I regard God's will as better than my will. I shall attach myself to Him as a servant and follower, my choice is one with His, my desire one with His, in a word my will is one with His will.'
Epictetus

Constantly think of the universe as one living creature, embracing one being and soul; how all is absorbed into the one consciousness of this living creature; how it compasses all things with a single purpose, and how all things work together to cause all that comes to pass, and their wonderful web and texture.
Marcus Aurelius IV.40

Stoicism presents a stand-alone system of faith in a "higher being" or "force" which leads to Stoicism's drive to make good character (virtue) and service to the greater good key to the living of life. The direction that science is taking us in regards understanding how the Universe is an interconnected whole that is permeated by some form of 'coordinating principle' that some scientists call 'the Consciousness' confirms much of the Stoic rationale regards the nature of the Cosmos.

"The stream of human knowledge is heading towards a non-mechanical reality. The universe begins to look more like a great thought than a great machine. Mind no longer appears to be an accidental intruder into the realm of matter. We are beginning to suspect that we ought rather to hail it as the creator and governor of this realm."
Sir James Jeans 1877 – 1946, an English physicist and astronomer, author of The Mysterious Universe

And from Sir James we also have:

"What remains is in any case very different from the full-blooded matter and the forbidding materialism of the Victorian scientist. His objective and material universe is proved to consist of little more than constructs of our own minds. .... Mind and matter, if not proved to be of similar nature, are at least found to be ingredients of one single system."

If a person has no interest in Stoicism other than for its therapeutic training aimed at achieving clarity of mind - that is fine. However, understanding the background of where the training is coming from will help to clarify some of the reasoning as to why matters are presented as they are. A lack of an understanding of the underlying Stoic principles can lead to a misunderstanding of the training that can then lead to something akin to the often-misguided cold-hearted Victorian application of some of the Stoic ideas, especially the mistaken aim of trying to suppress all emotions and any manifestation of inner feelings.

I am aware that among the ill-informed the Stoic school is unpopular on the ground that it is excessively harsh and not at all likely to give good counsel to princes and kings; the criticism is made that it does not permit a wise man to be pitiful, does not permit him to pardon. Such doctrine, if stated in the abstract, is hateful; for, seemingly, no hope is left to human error, but all failures are brought to punishment. And if this is so, what kind of a theory is it that bids us unlearn the lesson of humanity, and closes the surest refuge against ill-fortune, the haven of mutual help? But the fact is, no school is more kindly and gentle, none more full of love to man and more concerned for the common good, so that it is its avowed object to be of service and assistance, and to regard not merely self-interest, but the interest of each and all.
Seneca's Essays, 'On Mercy, II

It is also to be remembered that Stoicism is not an ancient dead philosophy frozen in time.

'The truth will never be discovered if we rest contented with discoveries already made. Besides, he who follows another not only discovers nothing, but is not even investigating… Men who have made these discoveries before us are not our masters, but our guides. Truth lies open to all; it has not yet been monopolised. And there is plenty left of it even for posterity to discover.'
Seneca 'On the futility of Learning Maxims'

Along with new discoveries comes new and better ways of explaining what Stoicism of old had set down as its 'principles' and this has affected some of the rationale that flowed from the metaphysics of old.

However, such restatement has not negated the overall thrust of the ideas that classical Stoicism offers us.

Stoicism is ultimately all about how, as individuals, we choose to use wisdom to live life in harmony with all about us. But, in that 'wisdom' is to be seen as 'the appropriate use of knowledge', to be true to Stoicism, we also have a need to look to the state of our knowledge today and so re-establish the core beliefs that, as Stoics, we use as a backdrop to all of our judgements, choices and actions in life.

This way we can be ready to adapt to circumstance, while having a firm foundation for our worldview – a foundation that will help us through both the good and the not so good times whereby we will remain true to our ethos while trying to serve all around us as best we can – which is after all what Stoicism is mostly about.

We can learn in these modern times from the observation of Nature, just as the ancients did, and we can look to where such observation leads regards teaching us how to live.

We can look to present day knowledge and follow the rationale that tells us about our place in the Universe and how we may be the 'best actors' we can possibly be when it comes to fulfilling our roles in the 'play of life'. We may not follow exactly the same course that the ancients followed in their understandings, but we will end up with a rationale that will be the same in intent as that presented in the extant Stoic writings from Greece and Rome.

Some details and explanations will alter, but the end product will be a sound cohesive set of Stoic ideas that will offer us 'a mode of conduct characterised by tranquillity of mind and certainty of moral worth' and that will guide us as to how we can live in harmony with Nature.

There is much repetition in these essays in that that is what they are – essays and writings produced at various times as a process of gathering together my thoughts on various aspects of Stoicism, thoughts that have sought to merge the ancient classic writings with the perspective of a Stoic who is alive in the twenty-first century. These writings are presented with an apology for the lack of skill and 'style' in authoring such essays. Finesse in grammar and rhetoric, which has always been an important part of the education system from ancient times right through to today, has always eluded me.

As an aside, it is popular in some circles to claim that Stoicism is sexist. It is true that most of the writings refer to 'man' but, in accord with the Stoic rationale, this is to be seen as generally referring to 'mankind' where the guidance is being given for all people - regardless of sex, or any other divisions of the human race.

1. Just who is this guy Zeno?

We are told that Zeno was a son of a trader who came from Citium, an ancient city on the island of what is today called Cyprus and we are told that two thousand three hundred years ago in Athens he set in place the foundations of a practical and spiritual school of thought that is effectively a 'user's manual' for the life that we have been born into.

We are told that Zeno studied the teachings that abounded in Athens (and probably many others from further afield) but in the end he was not satisfied that any of them offered a complete guide on how to live life and so he set about organising various thoughts and ideas into a single unified framework of ideas that he felt would offer any individual the chance of truly living life well.

The resultant framework evolved into what is now known as classic Stoicism.

I first came across Zeno in about 1989 through a small book that was a record of a lecture by Gilbert Murray (a classical scholar and Professor of Greek at Oxford University) which was originally presented at the South Place Institute in London on 16th March 1915 and was entitled 'The Stoic Philosophy'. In his lecture Murray tells us that Zeno wanted to know how to live but to answer this he needed to work out what to believe.

Demonstrating this, Zeno set the standard for 'how to live' as being 'to live in accord with Nature' – an aphorism that we are told is adopted by all Stoics (the followers of Zeno's teachings).

Zeno tells us that we can discover how we ought to be living by looking to what Existence (Nature) presents us with – a 'what you see is what you get' approach. And this not only involves seeing how events are physically unfolding before our eyes, but also involves having a framework of understanding regards the nature of Existence in its many guises, as well as an understanding of our place in the overall scheme of things.

In Zeno's time, in Greece, the study of the natural sciences was in its infancy, and without many of the study facilities available to us today much of such study involved speculation regards what could be observed through the senses – and of course, at times, such speculation could go wide of the mark or could be over-complicated as a result of the debate between the competing schools of philosophy at the time. But even so, Zeno came up with much that hit the mark and so offers an enduring understanding of the nature of the life humankind has been born into.

Despite the popularity of the new intellectualised ideas of his time that came out of the practice that professed to be driven by 'a love of wisdom' (philosophy), Zeno chose not to ignore the wisdom that had been passed down over the years, especially where such was seen to be common to most cultures.

By stripping away the myth and tradition from the beliefs of the various cultures he found that there were many 'common beliefs' that offered a sound understanding of the way things are. He examined these pieces of understanding to ensure that they could not be contradicted by simple observation of the world about us while ensuring that they fitted into and were of benefit to his overall 'big picture' that aimed to help a person to live well.

His was a wisdom approach rather than a purely scientific one.

He established a principle that any individual belief about the nature of life and how to live it had to fit like jigsaw pieces into an overall picture. That is, they had to be reasonable in that they did not negate some other aspect of the overall belief system, nor should they be contrary to what we experience through our senses in day-to-day living. The individual ideas have to make sense within the complete sphere of ideas that form the overall framework that is Stoicism.

And the end aim of Zeno's ideas was to enable the person in the street to have beliefs and standards that would enable them to live a life of contentment while striving to fulfil their roles in life as best and as appropriately as they can. Spiritual, personal and societal all at the same time.

Sounds simple enough, but success requires a degree of thoughtfulness and commitment. And such is helped by the fact that Zeno's teachings offered not only a manual on the structure of Existence and how to live life, but it also offered a simple faith that helped give purpose and direction to an individual's journey through life.

To restate what Murray pointed out, Zeno based all of his ideas about 'how to live' on what it is reasonable to believe. As such the starting point in following Zeno's methods has to be establishing an understanding of the nature of Existence and hence our nature as individuals and our place in life – we have to establish what we believe about the physics of Existence before we can establish the ethics by which we ought to live.

Many would-be Stoics today tend to reject the idea of the need to understand Zeno's view of the physics of Existence – mainly because they reject Zeno's theistic viewpoint or because they have come to Stoicism through reading certain populist books written over the last twenty years or so – books that effectively present Stoicism as nothing more than a self-help therapy for people with psychological issues.

As it is, I agree with Professor Gilbert Murray where he states that Stoicism may be defined both as a philosophy and a religion for it is not bound by the limitations of the 'scientific method'. We are not talking about proving anything to the nth degree – only, in light of observation, experience and the wisdom that has stood the test of time, as to if it is reasonable to believe that our inner experiences of life are as good a reflection of the realities of life as possible.

We are talking of an understanding of the nature of Existence that will guide us as to how we can best live life.

Professor Gilbert Murray tells us that Zeno (and hence Stoicism) makes assumptions when it is claimed that there is a beneficial purpose that drives the state of the world and that the 'force' that coordinates Nature as a whole is akin to us and the way we interact with what is around us. But he also tells us that the whole Stoic system 'falls easily into place' if we accept these assumptions.

In similar manner, more recently, another renowned expert on Stoicism, Anthony A Long, a classical scholar and Professor of Classics, in his book 'Stoic Studies' (1996 Cambridge University Press), arrives at the conclusion that any attempt to justify Stoic ethics fails if such does not include the Stoic understanding regards determinism and divine providence – he states that any such attempts would be 'broken backed'.

And, of course, the issues of determinism and providence within Zeno's teachings are an essential aspect of the Stoic view of the physics of life.

That is, the 'how to live' is what 'Stoic ethics' is about, and the 'what to believe' is what 'Stoic physics' is about, and so, looking to what Murray tells us, one cannot arrive at a Stoic view of ethics without first establishing a framework of understanding regards the nature of the physics of life.

As living as a Stoic involves 'living in accord with Nature' we need to be aware of the 'physical' nature of all around us. So today's Stoicism, to be Stoicism, needs to remain true to classic Stoicism, while also looking to advances in knowledge since the time of Zeno. As Seneca, the Roman statesman and a prominent Stoic tells us,

'The truth will never be discovered if we rest contented with discoveries already made. Besides, he who follows another not only discovers nothing, but is not even investigating... Men who have made these discoveries before us are not our masters, but our guides. Truth lies open to all; it has not yet been monopolised. And there is plenty left of it even for posterity to discover.'
Moral Essays XXXIII - On the futility of Learning Maxims

And:

We need to spend our time on study and on the authorities of wisdom in order to learn what has already been investigated and to investigate what has not yet been discovered.
CIV - On the care of Health and Peace of Mind

The Stoic today is not expected to accept blindly all that was written two millennia ago. However, Zeno had a particular way of viewing matters and if we are to have him and his followers in ancient Athens and Rome as our guides, and if we are to retain sufficient of the classical Stoicism to still be able to call any modern-day belief system Stoicism, we have a need to consider what Zeno would have made of much of the present-day discoveries and sciences.

Would he have arrived at different conclusions about the physics of life and, if so, would this have affected his ethical teachings? After all, as stated, ethics does not stand alone. It cannot be restated often enough, as Zeno recognised, ethics is about how one lives one's life and so ethics needs an understanding of the physical life one is living in in order to work out what is the ethical way to proceed.

There are clearly, from today's perspective, some aspects of the physics of life that the Stoics of old discussed that need to be amended or, even, rejected. But there are many aspects of the Stoic teachings that still ring true – hence the fact that many people still find that Stoicism offers something of benefit for today's seeker after a better life.

Zeno recognised that if a person is to benefit the most from Stoicism, there is a need to habituate one's beliefs as to the nature of Existence – we have to have faith. This way we Stoics do not just go through life with 'good intent', but we have an ingrained belief about how life works (a life manual) that helps us to habitually keep in mind 'the bigger picture' and so be more likely to make the right and proper choices in life – while adapting appropriately to the flow of change as life unfolds around us.

And so, to look to what Zeno would probably have made of the physics of life if he had been alive today, together with some other thoughts that stem from thinking like Zeno ....

2. Thinking like Zeno

It is said of Zeno that he saw that in order to know how to live he had to understand the nature of the Existence in which he lived. [Gilbert Murray a classical scholar and Professor of Greek at Oxford University. In his lecture which was originally presented at the South Place Institute in London on 16th March 1915]

This is confirmed by Zeno in that he set in place the Stoic prime guide for living life well: To live in accord with Nature.

It is acceptance of this aphorism, 'To live in accord with Nature', and all that the Stoic principles imply, that is the mark of what it is to be a Stoic.

'Meanwhile, I follow the guidance of Nature – a doctrine upon which all Stoics are agreed. Not to stray from Nature and to mould ourselves according to her law and pattern – this is true wisdom.'
Seneca On the Happy Life iii.

'To live according to virtue is the same thing as living according to one's experience of those things which happen by nature; .... Our individual natures are all parts of Universal Nature, and that means corresponding to one's own nature and to Universal Nature; doing none of those things which the common law of mankind is in the habit of forbidding, and that common law is identical with that right reason that pervades everything, being the same with Jupiter [God], who is the regulator and chief manager of all existing things. Again, this very thing is the virtue of the happy man and the perfect happiness of life when everything is done according to a

harmony with the genius of each individual with reference to the will of the universal governor and manager of all things.'
Diogenes Laertius LIII

The consequences of 'To live in accord with Nature' are foundational to Stoic thought and the rationale behind it tells us that we can only know how to live well if we have an understanding of the nature of the Existence that we find ourselves living in.

We have need to understand how individual aspects of Nature and how Nature as a whole influence, affects and even, to varying degrees, controls our individual lives if we are to have a hope of being anything more than 'puppets of the gods'.

To understand why this is Stoic 'policy' we need to understand Zeno's thinking and to understand why his thinking is not in conflict with advances in knowledge up to the present day.

Zeno was not a 'fatalist' in that he believed that we can influence how we live, that we can choose to live well and, on top of this, if we live well, we can, as a by-product, improve our state of 'eudaimonia'. We can bring about a state within ourselves whereby we can achieve the more or less permanent feeling that we are 'possessed of a good spirit' – this being the literal translation of the word 'eudaimonia'. The Stoic is not looking at that state called 'happiness' that is, according to its Middle-English origins, an emotional reaction to fleeting chance events. Rather, the Stoic looks to achieving 'good-spirits' where such is seen as a rational feeling of wellbeing and oneness with the rest of the Cosmos that is based on living in accord with a sound understanding of the realities of life.

Of course, it is not necessary to be aware of every minutia of Existence to achieve such. Nor do we need to prove things to the nth degree. Life is not something that can be, or should be, subjected to being 'lived in accord with the scientific method'.

What Zeno and what we Stoics are looking to is how Nature affects our lives on a day-to-day basis and how we cope with such. So, there are particular aspects of the nature of Existence that we do need to consider. As is to be seen throughout the history of mankind, some of these are foundational to our understanding of our place in the scheme of things. And only if we have an understanding regards our place in the scheme of things will we be able to truly assess how we should live.

When it comes to being a Stoic we look to the Stoic metaphysics.

In searching for what to believe, Zeno saw that he first needed to consider the overall nature of the Cosmos we live in as well as the nature of 'Zeus' (the supreme god of the ancient Greek culture) in relation to the Cosmos.

Barring one or two off-message individuals who fell by the wayside, Zeno and his followers are theists and, as Marcus Aurelius so eloquently expresses matters, for the Stoic there is a close correlation between the nature of the Cosmos and the nature of 'Zeus' whereby both are to be seen as *the universal governor and organiser of all things'*.

'We do not need to uplift our hands towards heaven… as if in this way our prayers were more likely to be heard. God is near you, he is with you, he is within you… The Holy Spirit indwells within us. One who marks our good deeds and our bad deeds, and is our guardian. Indeed, no man can be good without the help of God. … He it is that gives noble and upright counsel.'
Seneca XLI. On the God Within Us

"For I regard God's will as better than my will. I shall attach myself to Him as a servant and follower, my choice is one with His, my desire one with His, in a word my will is one with His will."
Epictetus IV.VII

'All things are mutually intertwined, and the tie is sacred, and scarcely anything is alien the one to the other. For all things have been ranged side by side, and together help to order one ordered Universe. For there is both one Universe, made up of all things, and one God immanent in all things, ... and one Law, one Reason common to all intelligent creatures, and one Truth.'
Marcus Aurelius VII.9

By looking to the views of the wise from many cultures and from many ages and by stripping such of tradition and myth, Zeno saw that there are common threads that are to be found in all of the world belief systems. And when it comes to 'Zeus', if one strips away the ancient Greek traditions and myth one finds the same common threads – this is why Stoicism came more to use the generic term God than 'Zeus' (God being the English translation of the Greek 'Theos' and the Latin 'Deus').

'Zeus' was no longer seen as being a god of human stature that lived in some Olympian domain. Instead, being seen as 'the one God', the Stoic deity becomes that state or force or consciousness common to all faiths, that is seen as being that which animates the Cosmos as a whole, together with all within it.

At the same time, based on beliefs from all over the world, the Stoic deity is seen to be the Cause of all that is, as having influence down to the level of the nature of how our planet operates as a bio-system, and even to having a relationship with us, the individual.

Where is the proof for such ideas? In part it lies in the innate feeling that there is 'a friend beyond phenomena' ['Stoics and sceptics' 1913, Edwyn Robert Bevan as referred to by Murray in his 1915 lecture] that is to be found in all of the people of the world. It is only by a great effort of denial driven by a human-centric sense of superiority that an individual can 'intellectually' reject this deep-rooted feeling.

Stoicism claims that these wisdoms have grounds for acceptance in that they are so widespread.

But Zeno did not just rely on the 'common beliefs' of humankind. He also looked to what it is reasonable to assume regards how the Cosmos is manifested.

In looking to all that they saw about them, Zeno and his followers saw the Cosmos as being a coordinated integrated system where reason dictates that things be as they are because there is a 'force' that causes everything to be as it is.

Diogenes Laertius tells us of the Stoic metaphysics:

They [the Stoics] think that there are two general principles in the universe, the active and the passive. That the passive is matter, an existence without any distinctive quality. That the active is the reason which exists in the passive, that is to say, God. For that he, being eternal, and existing throughout all matter, makes everything. And Zeno, the Cittiaean, lays down this doctrine in his treatise on Essence, and so does Cleanthes in his essay on Atoms, Chrysippus in the first book of his Investigations in Natural Philosophy, towards the end,

*Archedemus in his work on Elements, and Posidonius in the
second book of his treatise on Natural Philosophy.*
Diogenes Laertius LXVIII

*And they say that the substance of all existing things is
Primary Matter, as Chrysippus asserts in the first book of his
physics; and Zeno says the same. Now matter is that from
which anything whatsoever is produced. And it is called by a
twofold appellation, essence and matter; the one relating to
all things taken together and the other to things in particular
and separate. The one which relates to all things taken
together, never becomes either greater or less; but the one
relating to things in particular does become greater or less, as
the case may be.*
Diogenes Laertius LXXVI

Zeno presents us with a Cosmos that is absolutely physical in nature –
a strict materialism, but a materialism that is Stoic in nature in that the
'prime material' that, according to the Stoic rationale, fully fills the
Cosmos and is the body of the Cosmos, is seen to be imbued with the
mind of God. As Marcus Aurelius tells us, Stoicism involves a belief
in the 'one God immanent in all things.' All of the material existence
that we experience is, in a manner, 'conscious' and it is made manifest
as 'things' (individualities) through the very 'Consciousness' that
permeates the whole Cosmos. Zeno tells us that without such an
integral 'Consciousness'/God, the Cosmos would forever have been 'an
existence without any distinctive quality'.

There is much in today's modern sciences that offer grounds for these
and similar beliefs.

For Stoicism, God is all-encompassing. Seen as a whole, God is 'the universal governor and organiser of all things', but God can also be experienced as 'a friend' in the manner of Socrates' daemon.

As is reflected in the above quotes from some of the Roman Stoics, Stoics believe that God is integral to our lives and how we live them. If we take the knowledge of the nature of things and how they are aspects of the one living Cosmos permeated by God (Stoic physics) and align this with a suitable rationale (Stoic logic/reason) we will be guided as to how we ought to habitualise ourselves whereby we will live as good a life as we can, a life that reflects a good character (Stoic ethics).

In 'living in accord with Nature' the Stoic will live as the rational social animal that they are, in full knowledge that they are manifested out of the body of God, in that from our metaphysics we know that we are made out of the material that is the Cosmos and so contain within ourselves the 'two general principles' of the Cosmos. These are 'the active and the passive' where the 'active' is God, and as such we know, as Seneca tells us, that God is within us while at the same time we are, in a manner, a part of God. And knowing this, we Stoics try to live in a way that respects God while serving society as best that our roles in life, abilities and Fate will allow.

When it comes to serving society, we are told:

"The wise man… is born to be of help to all and to serve the common good."
Seneca 'On Mercy' II.vi

"Mankind have been created for the sake of one another."
Marcus Aurelius VIII.59

When it comes to the Stoic ethics, in order to 'live in accord with Nature', the Stoic aims to develop the four cardinal characters that are necessary to manifest a good character – Wisdom, Courage, Justice and Moderation.

The Stoic does not seek to manifest a good character for their own sake. Nor do they seek it in order to achieve the state of 'eudaimonia'. They seek to manifest a good character so that 'they will better act out their roles in the play of life in accord with the guidance of the Playwright and so benefit the overall progress of the play.'

As Seneca tells us:

"we must have a sound mind and one that is in constant possession of its sanity; second, it [the mind] must be courageous and energetic, and, too, capable of the noblest fortitude, ready for every emergency, careful of the body and of all that concerns it, but without anxiety; lastly, it must be attentive to all the advantages that adorn life – the user, but not the slave, of the gifts of Fortune."
'On the Happy Life' iii

And of course, the Stoic will use 'the advantages that adorn life' that come their way in a manner that will appropriately enable them to better 'live in accord with Nature' and so to better serve society.

In order to help the Stoic to live ethically in accord with their Stoic principles, Stoicism offers a full training program. The training has three purposes.

One is aimed at the would-be-Stoic or anyone with a troubled mind. This is mind training to help a person to look at life anew and to correct any adverse ingrained habits or thought processes and perceptions that are harmful to the individual's ability to cope with life – be it that such leads to a false overly negative or an overly positive view of life. We are enjoined by Marcus Aurelius [IV.11] to 'See things in all their naked reality.'

This training helps a person to regain a sound mind whereby they see life as it is and not through a filter of old misconceptions and it also helps the person to regain control of their emotions whereby their emotions will answer to the rule of reason. The training helps to prevent a person's emotions from triggering in an inappropriate manner or from running amuck and becoming excessive, violent and uncontrollable. This is the mind training part of the teachings that can be of use for the Stoic or non-Stoic.

But it is to be remembered that, contrary to popular modern belief, we Stoics do not eliminate emotions as part of our training. We ensure that our emotions and instincts serve us. Epictetus says at the start of his training program:

"but you have to give up some things entirely, and defer others for the time being."
Epictetus: The Encheiridion

And so it is to be seen that Epictetus' students in the closeted situation of Epictetus' school are guided to avoid all situations that elicit any emotional responses whatsoever - until such time as they have learnt which ones only needed to be deferred 'for the time being' in that the student has learnt how to keep them under control while at the same time having learnt which ones need to be 'given up entirely' – namely those such as anger - feelings that are excessive, violent and uncontrollable and will not answer to the rule of reason.

When it comes to appropriate emotions, Epictetus tells us that emotions such a love/affection for a spouse or a child are to be encouraged.

But for the present I can give you the following assistance toward the attainment of what you desire. Does family affection seem to you to be in accordance with nature and good? Of course. What then? Is it possible that, while family affection is in accordance with nature and good, that which is reasonable is not good? By no means. That which is reasonable is not, therefore, incompatible with family affection? It is not, I think. Otherwise, when two things are incompatible and one of them is in accordance with nature, the other must be contrary to nature, must it not?
Epictetus: XI 15 -23 'Of Family Affection'

When talking to a man who left his child's sick bed because he could not cope with his emotions, Epictetus argues that emotional feelings for family are natural and so are reasonable and to be encouraged and it is for the individual to ensure that their emotions are kept within bounds, and are expressed appropriately. Love for his child should have kept the man at his child's bed side.

The second area of training is the learning of the Stoic beliefs, metaphysics and how the actual physical nature of life will inform the Stoic as to how they ought to live their lives – Stoic theory and observation. For instance, a person learns what it is that they are aiming for when they aim to become a person of good character by looking to common opinion about what a good character is, and, if they are lucky enough to be able to do so, by observing and being in the company of people who demonstrate that they are possessed of an advanced good character. Another aspect is that a person learns to belong, in that they discover their place in the scheme of things, both in relation to God and also to the life they have been born into.

Both of these areas of training help the Stoic to know what is ethical.

In both of these areas of training, progress as a Stoic habituates Stoic ideas and ways of thinking to whereby such ideas and ways become second nature, while at the same time using the habituation of the new ways to also overcome and eliminate any old habitual ways of thinking and acting that are liable to block any progress.

And this is the final area of training. It is the ongoing lifelong process of reinforcement through habituation of the understandings that the other two areas of training will have brought about. Such habituation is achieved through ongoing study and revision regards the Stoic metaphysics and principles so as to reinforce our beliefs, together with regular self-assessments and corrections of our 'opinions' as necessary. And to cap off all of the training, the Stoic beliefs and way of life are reinforced by actually acting as a Stoic. Actual experience of physically living as a Stoic is the most powerful tool in our arsenal.

Act as you would be and you will be as you act.

Living as a Stoic is not about philosophising about how one ought to think, albeit that such helps. Living as a Stoic is all about our actions and how we physically, in full consciousness, live our lives for the benefit of the whole.

To some extent, we are not responsible for what thoughts and perceptions pop into our minds. We are responsible for what of these we assent to, in that what we assent to will play a part in how we interact with all around us. Our character, which the Stoic is encouraged to cultivate, is that which is to be seen through our outer demeaner and actions and, for a Stoic, a good character will be manifested as a result of following our reasoned choices that are supported by our Stoic belief system and worldview.

When talking of God, Stoicism talks of 'providence' and 'determinism'. That is, that God does not randomly manifest the Cosmos as it is out of the 'passive' nature of the 'prime matter', but rather that God manifests all within the Cosmos with purpose. When it comes to 'the big picture' we as individuals may not always be able to see such purpose, but Stoicism enjoins us to seek out the purpose of our own life as best we can.

As individuals that are manifested out of 'the body of God', we Stoics are guided to be attentive and ready to play our part in helping to 'determine' the flow of life with 'providence' (forethought) whereby we try to direct the flow of change where we can appropriately, partially or fully, influence matters towards the better.

Which is why the Stoic of good character will be the person who 'lives in accord with Nature' by striving to make their will *one with the will of God'* and who also lives up to being the rational responsible social animal that they are, with emphasis on the word 'social'.

And looking at the term 'rational', this relates to the word 'ratio' whereby the Stoic tries to consider the ratio of influence that all of the different aspects of their wisdom and acquired knowledge will bring to their judgements, opinions and choices – where foundational to this will be the Stoic beliefs, metaphysics and principles.

Stoicism is not solely about sorting out one's thought processes in order to achieve a sound mind. Overall Stoicism, as envisioned by Zeno, is a theistic belief system that is about physically living life honourably and appropriately in a manner that aligns one's will with the will of God – as Epictetus so clearly informs us.

By looking to how Zeno thought, we are able to take the advances in knowledge up to the present day and restate the reasonings behind much that Zeno offered us without changing Stoicism in any significant way.

If we are to ensure that we stay true to Zeno's vision, if we are to stay true to Stoicism, we have need to hold to the Stoic theistic metaphysics that says, as Marcus Aurelius tells us, that the Cosmos as a whole "is both one Universe, made up of all things, and one God immanent in all things" in that the Stoic metaphysics tells us that the Cosmos is manifested out of its 'prime constituent' and that the 'active principle' of this 'prime constituent' is God.

And it just so happens that the subatomic and quantum sciences of today present us with the need for a 'Consciousness' that permeates the whole Cosmos - if some of their theories are going to stand up to scrutiny. Modern science is beginning to catch up with the thoughts and reasonings of Zeno.

3. Against overly intellectualising the simplicity of the Stoic rationale

Zeno and his followers were caught up in the Athenian intellectual arena whereby every aspect of the teachings of any of the schools of thought were gone over with a fine-tooth comb. As such, the simplicity of the rationale of Zeno's teachings tended to be overlooked. Every aspect had to be defined and explained in ever greater detail in order to counter the assault by the intellectuals of the other schools.

While there was a serious aspect to the teachings of the various schools, to a great extent 'the love of wisdom' became a mind game for those who saw themselves as members of a society of what would today be called the 'intelligentsia'.

In recent years professors of academic Philosophy and professors of the Classics have tried to collate what is known of Zeno's teachings. In that they have tried to present their ideas based on what original writings are still available today and in that what writings there are that can be attributed to those of the Stoic school are thin on the ground, they have looked to other schools and commentators of the time to try to flesh out what they believe is the technical detail behind much of the Stoic ideas.

All of their work is to be applauded, but being academic professors, they are often seeing Stoicism as a subject matter that needs to be critically assessed against their modern academic standards. However, in that Stoicism is a faith-based belief system, academic analysis is not necessarily the best way for a would-be Stoic to approach the subject, albeit that some of the academic writings can provide some useful background and understanding of the climate in which Zeno thought through his ideas.

But once the would-be-Stoic has achieved an understanding of the background ideas, they are best served by moving on from treating it as an intellectual 'subject of interest.' Instead, the Stoic looks to Stoicism as a spiritual faith and a practical guide to living life whereby our path is best served by knowing our place in the scheme of things and through understanding that we are manifested out of 'the body of God' - and so learning how to be a good person.

And here, starting from the Stoic belief in the nature of the Deity, the Stoic rationale leads the Stoic on to the simplicity of what it is to serve society and the Cosmos.

As an example of the simplicity of the Stoic rationale, we are told that all we need to do to know how a person aiming to be of good character should act is to look to the 'common perceptions' of humankind that tell us what it is to be a good person. And, through this method, even the 'bad' person recognises what it takes to be a good person.

Of course, at times people can view matters through tinted glasses. Which is why another simple aspect of the Stoic rationale is to see life as it really is and not as we or our emotions may wish to see it.

Stoicism involves many simple ideas that are to be seen to combine with other ideas that the Stoic rationale throws up. This offers a rational understanding as to how to deal with any situation one may encounter in life. One simple observation of the nature of an aspect of life, combined with many other simple observations, sometimes based on a different point of view, will lead to an understanding of what is appropriate regards the individual's input into the moment by moment living of the life they have been born into.

We look to the nature of things in order to learn how to live and, in that things are forever changing, we also maintain an element of awareness as to the need to be ready to adapt to circumstance while also looking to the wisdom that has been passed down over the ages – wisdom that may guide us with the voice of experience.

As a result, we are accepting of what life throws at us, including loss and death in that these are aspects of the nature of things. Step by step we follow the simple rationale of the Stoic study of the nature of things to ensure that we are able to be accepting of the realities of life whereby any natural feelings/emotions will remain proportionate to any situation that triggers them, so avoiding them becoming 'perturbations' that divert us from our aim to be good and to 'live in accord with Nature'.

There is nothing complicated about the Stoic teachings. Nothing is complicated or counter intuitive. There is no need for some academic level of study. Stoicism is simplicity itself in that it is grounded in the common beliefs of the world faiths and it looks to the 'common perceptions' of humankind for guidance. All that is needed to learn what the Stoic life involves is a mind that is capable of a level of sound thought together with an element of self-discipline.

All that Stoicism asks of us is that we choose to align our will with the will of God (that we 'live in accord with Nature'), which involves us trying as best we can to be aware of what our sense 'impressions' of the world are telling us while also being as aware as possible as to what the consequences of our chosen actions are liable to be on the whole, be they intentional consequences or otherwise. To this end we try to live in a manner that is, for the good person, appropriate and of benefit to the wellbeing of all around us according to circumstance. And sometimes that means looking to the bigger picture and putting what may be seen as our own self-interests to one side.

The Stoic's selfish self-interest is served through living selflessly.

4. Stoic understanding and understanding Stoicism

The Stoicism that Zeno founded is not laid out in great detail as a 'cast in stone' 'this is the way things are' system of thought. There is no 'Stoic Bible'. Any given issue is addressed by following the rationale that follows from the basic Stoic principles.

The basic Stoic principles comprises the beliefs that:

Existence as a whole is physically real and knowable despite the flow of change that we experience throughout life. Therefore, existence is seen as being organised as against being chaotic. Any apparent chaos is just the result of our limitations regards being able to be aware of the overall cause of whatever we are viewing. For the whole of existence to be knowable and to not be chaotic it must hold together as a whole and so must be a singular material state – that is we experience existence as the Cosmos, where 'cosmos' is seen to refer to the Universe seen as a well-ordered whole.

With existence being organised, there has to be some form of 'organising principle'. In order to maintain the knowability across the whole Cosmos this 'organising principle' must permeate the whole Cosmos and must influence and coordinate all aspects of the Cosmos. In order to influence and coordinate all aspects of the Cosmos the 'organising principle' must be a singular state. This 'organising principle' is seen to be akin to what we call 'consciousness', where the 'organising principle' is the conscious nature that permeates the Cosmos - as is to be seen today in theories about the subatomic and quantum level of existence.

In that in Stoicism the Cosmos is seen to be 'the whole and the all' of everything that exists, there is no domain other than the Cosmos. The 'organising principle' is an inherent property of the Cosmos that causes the 'material' and 'forces' that manifest as the Cosmos to manifest as they do and as such the 'organising principle' is part of the overall nature of the Cosmos and is not external to the Cosmos.

The organising principle, the overall consciousness of the Cosmos, is seen to be one and the same as that which the world beliefs call the creative deity or force that is central to their faith. As such, the organising principle as seen through the Stoic principles is seen to be God, a god that has no form other than that of the whole Cosmos. The Cosmos is seen to be 'the body of God'.

Existence is seen as the flow of change that happens in the present moment. Consciousness at all levels of Existence is seen to be the cause of all change and such change happens only in the present moment though conscious in-the-moment determinism and/or through 'momentum' where momentum is the ongoing rational flow of aspects of Existence that have to comply with the laws of Nature. As such, being the overall conscious state of the Cosmos, God is ever present and immanent. And God, together with us as part of God, determines the direction of the ongoing flow of change, while always being limited as to what change is possible by the laws of Nature - these being part of the fundamental physical nature of the Cosmos. God cannot go against the laws of Nature in that they are part of the nature of the Cosmos.

As a result of the oneness of the Cosmos and the oneness of the consciousness that moulds it, so all of Existence, including ourselves, are part of this oneness. We are 'the children of God', and out of respect for God we ought to try to live up to this fact by trying to live in harmony with all around us. To 'live in harmony with Nature' is the call of all Stoics, where Nature is seen as being what we experience of the Cosmos as it is manifested through its physical nature and its conscious nature.

Being the children of God lays on us the responsibility to act in a manner that is of benefit to all, only looking to our own self-interest in so far as it enables us to be useful to the whole. That is, we aim to be citizens of the Cosmos that contribute to the overall wellbeing of the existence we find ourselves living in – as best as our circumstance, nature and ability will allow.

We learn about how we ought to live by looking to the nature of the world we have been born into and by looking to the common ideas of humankind regards such matters as to what, for example, is generally seen to be the way a loving parent should be regards their child, or a loving spouse ought to be regards their other half, etcetera. We learn about how we ought to be as family members, members of society and so on by looking to what is wise, just, courageous and appropriate – what are seen as the four cardinal values of a person of 'good character'.

In order not to be misled by our own selfish survival inclinations that are part of our nature as human animals, we are guided to train ourselves (and to keep to an ongoing training regime) to try to ensure that all of our instincts, feelings and emotions answer to the rule of our ability to reason rationally. This is not to say that we must suppress the feeling side of our nature, just that we have need to ensure that our feelings do not get out of hand and so do not lead us blindly into ways that are not in keeping with us living wisely and ways that are not in accord with our Stoic principles. The surrender of our rational self-control to excessive and aggressive feelings such as anger, is to be avoided as best as possible. As is the surrender of rational self-control to excessive or inappropriate feelings of aggressive 'love', where inappropriate desires for people or objects or incorrectly perceived benefits and the like are to be avoided.

In order to understand what is appropriate or not, we are guided to take care to examine the reality of what we perceive through our senses, which includes our ability to reason. (Reasoning is, in Stoicism, seen to be on a par with our other five physical senses.) Such examination is necessary in that all of our senses can mislead us. So we are guided to be as attentive to life as we can be and to have so habituated our thoughts that where we act out of habit, such habit will hopefully produce an appropriate response. We are guided, through learning and training, to try to eliminate all inappropriate past ways and habituations and to replace them with new more appropriate ways of acting.

All of the forgoing are to be seen as being the Stoic principles in that they are arrived at by the equivalent of 'reverse engineering' from the few Stoic writings and ancient commentaries that have survived the last two millennia, in that we have little or nothing of Zeno's own words in the present day. At the same time none of the above is contradicted by the advances in knowledge relating to the modern sciences and psychology. In fact, the question of 'the consciousness' is to be found in quantum science and the issue of training to look at reality in order to get our emotions into a state of stability is the very foundation of modern-day therapies such as CBT and REBT.

In many respects Stoicism was way ahead of its time and, as a result, it is still as relevant today as it was when Zeno first formulated its principles into a single system.

Individual Influence

Stoicism tells us that we are to 'live in accord with Nature'. However, part of Nature is our own individual nature, the nature we are born with as well as our nature that has been developed as a result of our nurture as children; be that 'children' who have not got through puberty - or – adult 'children' that have not 'grown up' in that they have chosen not to take responsibility for how their lives impinge on all around them.

'Living in accord with Nature' has two consequences. We have need to consider how our individual nature will influence how we develop our understanding of how to live life in harmony with all around us, while still following the rationale that is led by the Stoic principles. We also have need to consider which aspects of our nature need to be developed or 'tamed' in order that we may better serve the whole.

As such, Stoicism becomes individualistic for each one of us, in that as we take on board the Stoic principles so our developing rationale will be coloured by our own personality.

As a result, when it comes to the writings we have from of old, we need to be aware of the personal input of the various writers involved so that we can see past their personal interpretations to the core Stoic teachings to which they all subscribed.

The key figures to which most of today's professorial scholars turn in order to present us with an understanding of Stoicism are: Zeno, Cleanthes, Chrysippus, Panaetius, Posidonius, Cicero, Seneca, Musonius Rufus, Epictetus, Marcus Aurelius and Diogenes Laertius. These all lived between about 334BCE and 300AD. There were many more Stoics from whom we have little or no records and also many 'commentators' or 'critics' of Stoicism who had access to books we do not have today. Looking to the key figures who came after Zeno:

Cleanthes, the immediate successor to Zeno in the Stoic school in Athens, was from Asia Minor (near to what was Troy) and he lived from about 330BCE to 230BCE. His take on Stoicism was very much centred in looking to our relationship with God, as is exampled by his 'Hymn to Zeus'. He tended to stick closely to how Zeno presented Stoicism - as a practical and spiritual philosophy of life for the person in the street. It is notable that many of the early leaders of the Athenian Stoa were also from the eastern end of the Mediterranean and so also had a grounding in the theistic faiths that abounded in that area.

Chrysippus (c. 280 – 207BCE) was born in what is today Mersin in southern Turkey. He is considered by many today as having been an important figure in the 'development' of Stoicism, having written hundreds of books on numerous subjects. However, some of what he 'added' to the Stoic teachings have over time proved to be problematic. He contributed much on various subjects, including logic, that is still of interest today, but generally it is possible that he was trying to compete intellectually with the other Greek schools of thought at the time, whereas Zeno and Cleanthes' efforts appear to suggest that Stoicism was trying to pull back from purely intellectual competition and instead were offering practical solutions to the issues of the day – issues that we are still faced with in the modern era.

The next heads of the Stoa were Zeno of Tarsus, Diogenes of Babylon and Antipater of Tarsus – more individuals from lands at the eastern end of the Mediterranean, so setting Stoicism as being based in the Athenian tradition of philosophical discussion but with the added attraction of the Stoic theism – a theism that clearly appealed to those from further east.

Panaetius (C 185 – 110 BCE) from Rhodes (a Greek island off the eastern reaches of mainland Greece) was a student of Diogenes of Babylon and Antipater of Tarsus. For a period, he moved to Rome and together with others brought Stoicism to the Romans, with special emphasis on 'duties' – a subject that appealed to the Roman culture. He is described as being 'eclectic' in that he not only followed Stoicism as his main philosophy, but also looked to Plato and Aristotle in various areas, possibly because he did not have the more eastern theistic influence in that he was a Greek and so would have been more inclined to the older Athenian philosophies and the pantheon of Greek gods.

Posidonius (C 135 – 50BCE), also of Rhodes, followed on from Panaetius and was also seen as being 'eclectic' and to some extent, in some areas, he offered ideas that were contrary to what Chrysippus had offered. Both Posidonius and Panaetius are 'credited' with 'Romanising' Stoicism in that they emphasised Stoic ideas that would appeal to the Roman culture, especially those that talked of the duty of the individual to support the State.

Cicero (106 – 43 BCE) was a Roman statesman, orator, lawyer and philosopher. He was not a declared Stoic, but did offer translations into Latin and interpretations of a number of the Greek philosophical schools and, in the process, he showed a good understanding of Stoicism and so his writings add to the limited extant writings that offer us what we still have of the original classic Stoicism. Diodotus the Stoic (C 130 – 59BCE) lived in Cicero's house and is credited with teaching Cicero about Stoicism.

Seneca the Younger (C 4BCE – 65AD), born in Spain, was a Stoic philosopher and a Roman statesman. In his time, he tried to teach Nero (with emphasis on the word 'tried'). For about five years Seneca and the praetorian prefect Sextus Afranius Burrus ruled the Roman Empire on behalf of the young Nero, only for Seneca to be forced into retirement when others turned Nero against him. It is claimed that during the five years that Seneca and Sextus were in control, the Roman Empire was well managed, unlike the following years of Nero's rule. In keeping with his beliefs, when Nero turned against him, Seneca demonstrated his Stoic lack of attachment to his wealth by handing it over to Nero while requesting that he be allowed to retire to a small country estate, which is where he was when eventually he was forced to commit suicide on the orders of Nero.

Seneca's writings are fairly extensive and are presented in the form of essays and letters, all of which are written in Latin and offer a practical understanding of the Stoic teachings. In general, his writings offer much useful understanding as to what Stoicism involves as a way of life.

Musonius Rufus was a Roman born Stoic who lived in the first century AD and is best known as the Stoic teacher whose lectures were attended by Epictetus. There are some extracts of his lectures still available.

Epictetus (C 55 – 135 AD) was a freed Roman slave, who was born in present day Turkey. After being exiled from Rome, Epictetus set up a 'school for sick souls' in Nicopolis in north western Greece where he taught young men the Stoic teachings as he saw them. It is clear that his early life as a slave influenced how he taught Stoicism. We have none of his own writings. What we have are four out of eight books that are the 'notes' of one of his students who was called Arrian and we also have a book called the 'Enchiridion' or 'Manual of Epictetus'. These books are often the inspiration that brings people to the study of Stoicism in the present day.

Marcus Aurelius (121 – 180AD) was a Roman Emperor known as the last of 'the five good Emperors'. He is remembered in Stoicism for his diarised considerations of his Stoic beliefs that are known now as his 'Meditations' – a book that is also a great inspiration for many today.

Diogenes Laertius of the third century AD is described as a biographer of the various Greek philosophers. These biographies are found in a number of books called 'The Lives and Opinions of Eminent Philosophers'. Book seven covers the Stoics and the Stoic beliefs. While today some question his ability as a biographer, Diogenes had access to much of the original books and writings of the early Stoics – many of which are no longer available to us of the modern era, so his writings are an important contribution to the understanding of the Stoic principles.

So, at all times, in studying Stoicism, it needs to be remembered that what writings we have are the writings of men, tinged with their personalities, and that none are 'the word of God'. None of the Stoics of old are offering us the ultimate word in Stoicism – they are merely individuals who are offering their personal opinions as to where the rationale that starts with the Stoic principles leads us.

The writings we have are only those that survived to the present day. So Seneca, Epictetus and Marcus Aurelius are nothing more than three Stoics from whom we have any quantity of writings and that offer us their opinions as individuals – individuals who are not necessarily any more gifted in Stoic thought than anyone else who has spent time studying it. Each in their own way tried to live as Stoics. We each can do likewise if we, like them, study what we can of the principles that Zeno laid down and then try to put such into practice by following the rationale that such leads us to.

No past Stoic is our master. They are not even our teacher. They are all simply fellow students.

Even Zeno is only a fellow student in that he learnt from those who went before him and the originality that makes him the founder of Stoicism is in how he pulled together existing wisdoms and organised them into a new rational system that was aimed at the ordinary citizen, whereby Stoicism offers a simple understanding of our relationship to the divine as well as a practical understanding of how to address life.

Even though Zeno himself got caught up in the competition with other Athenian schools that had him and his followers talking of the impossible 'sage' and of 'eudaimonia', the underlying discovery that Zeno made was that the real aim of the 'good person' is to seek to live well as part of the Cosmos through 'living in harmony with Nature', where our observance of Nature is the window into understanding 'the will of God' in that Nature is all that we see around us and is the physical manifestation of the living conscious Cosmos.

Stoicism does not aim for some form of 'happiness' as the other Athenian schools did. Zeno realised that we have to set aside such aims and instead aim to be 'good people' who work to be of benefit to all around us. If we find peace and contentment along the way, all well and good. But Zeno shows that we will only find such, as Stoics, if we can be confident that we have lived as best as we can. And living well is open to all. As Seneca says,

'Do you know why we have not the power to attain the Stoic Ideal? It is because we refuse to believe in our power. Nay, of a surety, there is something else which plays a part: it is because we are in love with our vices; we uphold them and prefer to make excuses for them rather than shake them off... The reason is unwillingness, the excuse, inability.'
CXVI. On Self Control

All we need in order to be 'good people' is to choose to be 'good people' – and Stoicism offers a framework of principles that will enable us to achieve such.

OK, at times we may get matters wrong, but that is part of our nature as human beings. So regardless of the fact that we will not achieve our target all the time, when we do miss the target, we have no excuse to not pick ourselves up, dust ourselves off, and move on in our quest to be as good as we can, as much as we can. That is all that is asked of the Stoic – all that is asked is that we try as earnestly as we can to 'live in harmony with Nature' and so to seek to make our will one with the will of God (as Epictetus repeatedly tells us).

5. In Support of Zeno's Metaphysics

What follows is an amalgamation of a number of individual posts and essays written over a number of years – so again, apologies for any repetition. The essays are an attempt to look to where the rationale of the Stoic metaphysics of old takes us when considered against a rationale that considers the input of knowledge from the modern sciences. Any theorising regards such modern knowledge is unashamedly influenced by the classic Stoic view and does not necessarily follow the 'orthodox' scientific theorising.

Existence

They [the Stoics] think that there are two general principles in the universe, the active and the passive. That the passive is matter, an existence without any distinctive quality. That the active is the reason which exists in the passive, that is to say, God. For that he, being eternal, and existing throughout all matter, makes everything. And Zeno, the Cittiaean, lays down this doctrine in his treatise on Essence, and so does Cleanthes in his essay on Atoms, Chrysippus in the first book of his Investigations in Natural Philosophy, towards the end, Archedemus in his work on Elements, and Posidonius in the second book of his treatise on Natural Philosophy.
Diogenes Laertius, LXVIII

And they say that the substance of all existing things is Primary Matter, as Chrysippus asserts in the first book of his physics; and Zeno says the same. Now matter is that from which anything whatsoever is produced. And it is called by a twofold appellation, essence and matter; the one relating to all things taken together, and the other to things in particular

and separate. The one which relates to all things taken
together, never becomes either greater or less; but the one
relating to things in particular does become greater or less, as
the case may be.
Diogenes Laertius LXXVI

Here we are looking at how Stoicism claims Existence is made manifest here and now. Not how it is supposed that it came into existence by some magician type god 'pulling it out of an empty hat' in a moment of 'creation'. Instead, we are looking to how it exists as a flow of change from one moment to another. And in this respect Zeno settled on a 'theory' that is not too dissimilar to ideas that can be arrived at by looking to disciplines such as quantum science and other ideas that scientists are presenting us with today.

We are told [The New Scientist 2nd Feb 2019 page 28 'What is Life' by Paul Davies, professor of physics at Arizona State University] that scientists are recognising the equation:

$$Life = Matter + Information$$

Where 'information' is seen as a 'physical quality' that changes the nature of 'material' from inanimate to animate.

Taking into account the Laws of Nature, it is a small step to the equation:

$$Existence = Matter + Information$$

Or in Stoic terms:

The Cosmos = the Passive quality of Matter + the Active quality of Matter

Where 'the active is the reason which exists in the passive, that is to say, God.'

Back in Zeno's time there was a debate between the Stoics and the Epicureans. The Epicureans effectively claimed that all of material existence was made out of 'atoms' that were seen as being the smallest possible building blocks of all that exists. They effectively saw 'atoms' as being akin to individual 'balls' that bounced around randomly and just happened to produce the world we see about us. Their view was the same as some scientists in the twentieth century that claimed that the Universe as we experience it is just the result of 'an accidental blip of organisation in a sea of chaos.'

Whereas the classic Stoicism of Zeno tells us that there is a stage beyond 'atoms' and 'the elements' and that at this level a 'prime matter' manifests everything from subatomic particles right up to the 'Universe' itself through the fact that there is a pan-universe 'God like' quality that animates the 'prime matter' – a quality without which Existence would be 'without any distinctive quality'. Contrary to the Epicurean view, Stoicism claims that Existence is not a random state, but is 'governed' by reason and rationality (or even 'information') whereby the Universe holds together as a single whole.

Nowadays, science tells us that 'atoms' are in fact made up of yet smaller pieces of 'matter' called 'particles' and that these subatomic particles do not operate as 'a random sea of chaotic activity' but in fact their activity is in some way the result of 'probability' and that there are what are theorised as being 'fields' that permeate the whole of the Universe and that impart qualities/information to all of the individual particles. (This is of course an over simplification of what is a vastly complicated view.)

At the same time, we are told that, in some scientific experiments, many of these physical 'particles' of matter do not always act as pieces of solid 'matter' but will at times act as if they are more like a 'wave' whereby the 'wave' will only show up as a 'particle' of 'solid matter' if it is 'observed'.

Taking into account other aspects of what modern sciences is telling us, the rational conclusion of such is that the totality of the 'matter' that is the Cosmos is in some manner self-observing. Of course, we need to recognise that Zeno would now, in light of the advances in knowledge, consider that what he originally recognised as 'prime matter' needs to be recognised as being some form of 'self-observing energy' – an energy that possesses the qualities of passive and active as originally envisaged by Zeno.

Whereas the prime matter of old referred to a finer matter out of which the 'four elements' were manifested, this 'prime energy' may now be considered to be a self-observing sea of prime energy that fills and comprises the volume that is Space. In fact, there is little to differentiate between the original Stoic 'science' and today's theorising.

When talking of the four elements Zeno considered them all to be qualities of 'matter', being the qualities of solid, liquid, gaseous and energy – or as they are normally called, 'earth, water, air and fire' with fire being the 'finest' of the 'four elements.' However, Zeno envisaged that there had to be something finer than fire itself, this being the prime element out of which all four of the elements, including fire, were manifested. For want of another term, Zeno called this element 'divine fire' in that for it to manifest all else it had to be, in some manner, conscious and self-observing. So, in today's terms Zeno would probably talk of 'divine energy'.

In that Zeno saw that the four elements, which included fire, were all made out of a finer state, he would recognise that subatomic particles, forces and energy are seen as being built out of energy waves, whereby, in some manner, it may be considered that there is a 'prime energy' that manifests all else, this 'prime energy possibly being the medium through which energy waves are seen to propagate (move), even in deep space far from any other influence. Such a medium is not recognised by today's science in that any evidence of such is probably being laid at the door of the theorist's fabled 'Big Bang' theory rather than seeing such evidence for what it is.

While all of this new science (the last 100 years or so) is confusing for many of us, what comes out of it is that Stoicism was some 2000 years ahead of its time when it comes to understanding how Existence is manifested here and now, albeit that some of the ancillary Stoic theories of old need to be clarified in order to follow the advances in knowledge regards the physical world.

Now, in Zeno's days the Greeks saw the Universe as being no more than Planet Earth with the Sun, Moon and planets circling it within fairly close proximity. So it was reasonable to see all of this as being the manifestation of 'matter' imbued with some form of coordinating 'intelligence', akin to the properties often attributed to 'God', whereby the Universe is seen as the body of 'a single living creature' governed by 'one mind', so leading to the belief that the small Universe as envisaged by the ancient Greeks is to be seen as the 'body of the one God'.

Today's knowledge of the vastness of the Universe demands a restating of such ideas.

We hear talk of 'master programs' that coordinate imagined universes within computer programs and games. We talk of 'artificial intelligence' whereby computer programs operate in a manner that achieve something akin to what we would recognise as learning which leads to reasoned and rational output through the various interfaces with such Artificial Intelligence programs.

So it is clear that we are now able to recognise that there are non-human states that are capable of 'intelligently' manipulating and coordinating aspects of Existence. And if we can see such in animals and in machines etcetera, why not some form of 'master intelligence' that coordinates and manages the manifestation of the Universe as a whole?

The scientists are able to envisage a Universe wide 'field' that instantaneously imparts the quality of mass to various individual subatomic particles right across the whole of Space. (A process that is not limited by the speed of light). There is no reason to not consider that such a 'field' could be just a small part of an overarching system of coordination and enforcement of the laws of nature whereby the laws are applied and enforced in every corner of the Universe at every moment.

In fact, such 'laws' would not be 'laws' unless there is some property that permeates the whole Universe that ensures that the 'laws' are enacted as appropriate and wherever needed. Without some such 'master intelligence' or 'imparter of information' there would be nothing but 'an existence without any distinctive quality'.

Now, it may be seen as being a long stretch of the imagination seeing such a 'master intelligence' as being 'the God' (that so many faiths see as being involved in guiding and showing an interest in the human race). However, without a singular 'master intelligence' the Universe would not be able to form into the coordinated state that it is. The Universe would not be knowable, for a Universe not governed by a 'master intelligence' would not provide any consistency from one moment to the next. Cause and effect at the most basic of levels could not be relied on.

Of course, while science and logic dictate that such a 'master intelligence' must exist, its full nature will probably remain just speculation. But science is showing, that there exists a 'master intelligence' and purveyor of 'Information' that permeate the whole Universe and as such the Universe is the Cosmos in that 'Cosmos', by definition, is the Universe seen as 'a well ordered whole'.

Much of modern cosmology is based on what we can see of 'the visible universe' – so limiting us to a similar vision of the extent of the Cosmos that the ancient Greeks were limited to, only today we can 'see' so much further with the aid of technology. But regardless, our science-based knowledge is still limited to what is observable as our planet spins on its axis or as is visible from within the solar system in which our planet exists.

Our knowledge of the size of the Cosmos is at present limited by the speed of light and the vast expanse of Space. We 'see' a 'Universe', but it is clear that it is not rational to assume that the 'Universe' we 'see' reflects the extent of the Cosmos in which we exist. And as such, in that there are limits to what we can observe, we cannot set limits to the Cosmos or to the extent and the involvement of the 'master intelligence' that permeates it – namely God.

For all intents and purposes, from the human perspective, the Cosmos is infinite and eternal. At the same time our experience of its physical nature is the result of the 'master intelligence' manifesting all that is around us – very much as a 'master program' will manifest an 'existence' in which a computer game is played.

If the Cosmos as a whole was not made rational by the input of the 'master intelligence', way down in the scale of size, we humans would not be able to be the 'gamers' in 'the game of life' that we are. As said, without the 'master intelligence' there would just be 'an existence without any distinctive quality' – and that means there would be no 'us'.

From all that we now know, the fact that we exist within the Cosmos and that it holds together in a knowable manner whereby we are able to see out our 'three score years and ten,' demonstrates that it is a rational Cosmos governed by a 'master intelligence' – or as originally viewed by the Stoics, the Cosmos is made manifest by

'the universal governor and organiser of all things'
Diogenes Laertius LIII

And what else is this than that which is behind every World Faith – known to some by the appellation 'God' or 'the One God' – being that which is responsible for manifesting the Existence that we are part of.

Our Stoic view of God is not of a God being involved in some imagined 'point of creation' whereby the Universe suddenly came into being, but of a God that is the Cosmos and that is the very cause of the Cosmos appearing as it does.

God, the 'master intelligence', as perceived by Stoicism, manifests all that exists around us moment by moment and so is ever present. God did not light the blue touch paper and retire to a safe distance to watch the effects of some 'big bang' firework. God has been with us all along, and still is with us for we exist within the body of God.

This Stoic belief in the Cosmos as the body of God together with believing that the Cosmos is being manifested moment by moment by the 'master intelligence' that is God is key to developing and understanding the rationale of the whole Stoic framework.

Marcus Aurelius, the Stoic Roman Emperor, tells us:

'Cease not to think of the Universe as one living Being, possessed of... a single Soul; and how all things trace back to a single sentience; and how it does all things by a single impulse.'
Marcus Aurelius IV. 40

This is the foundational faith of Stoicism:

The Cosmos is a singular living physical Being, that is imbued with a 'master intelligence' that is God and that is 'the universal governor and organiser of all things' and as such the Cosmos and everything within the Cosmos is the body of God. And reason therefore tells us that we are one with God – we are all the children of God – for we are manifested out of God's body. And this translates into ethics in that we then understand that as individuals we ought to live up to the standards incumbent on us as 'the children of God' and as 'citizens of the Cosmos'.

On the Nature of Existence

In order to understand the nature of the life we have been born into we need to have some idea as to how things work. And for this, the starting point is to have a concept that guides us to an understanding of the very nature of Existence. This may seem a bit over the top and an ask-too-much for someone who is just trying to get on with life as best they can. But in that all of the guidelines presented to us by Zeno relate back to the nature of the Cosmos, if we want to be Stoics, this is where we need to start in order to achieve any real understanding of what is the best we can each individually achieve regards living a Stoic life of harmony.

We need to look to the big picture if we are to understand how we are to best fit in with life as a whole. We need to understand how things work in order to be able to follow what Zeno called 'the smooth flow of life'. And to do this we need a concept as to what that ultimate state of existence is, namely the Cosmos as a whole.

So here goes:

One of the basic principles in Stoicism is "Live in accord with Nature". What this means becomes apparent as one studies the whole of Stoicism. But starting with the largest aspect of the Cosmos, namely itself as a whole, we have Marcus Aurelius [Meditations, iv. 40] talking of its nature as follows:

"Constantly regard the universe as one living being, having one substance and one soul; and observe how all things have reference to one perception, the perception of this one living being; and how all things act with one movement; and how all things are the cooperating causes of all things that exist; observe too the continuous spinning of the thread and the structure of the web."

So what is the modern day Stoic to believe about this 'universe' that is "one living being, having one substance and one soul" in light of the advances in science, especially todays scientific cosmology and the subatomic and quantum sciences.

The ancients' view of the Cosmos was mostly based on the 'universe' being little bigger than this planet of ours with all the other 'lights' circling it in the sky – hence the Latin word 'universe', the root of which means 'one turn' or 'one cycle'. The 'universe' of the ancients was Planet Earth and the visible sky that revolved around it. (And yes, the Stoics understood that our planet is a sphere floating in space long before all the hoo-hah about the idea of a 'flat earth'.)

The ancient Greeks believed that all 'things' that exist are made up out of a mixture of the then recognised four elements of Earth, Water, Air and Fire, mixed in differing proportions according to the nature of what was being examined. These elements may be seen to represent what we would today call the states of solid, liquid, gaseous and energy - that is, they are the characters of material 'things' that we perceive through our senses.

The root of the word 'element' may be translated as 'first principle'. While modern ideas may make the idea of 'the four elements' as the building blocks of all 'things' look outdated, it is mainly because in science we now use the word 'element' to talk of different types of chemical atoms rather than as the character of the manifested state of anything. However, looked at as 'first principles' even the term chemical 'elements' may be seen as outmoded and we have to go beyond the atom to the subatomic world and the quantum world as the scientific community pushes back the boundaries and discover new 'first principles'.

Now the remarkable thing about Stoicism is that, despite the limitations of the ancient Greek world view, many of the Stoic conclusions about the nature of the Cosmos still hold, albeit on a larger scale than originally envisaged. So the question is, how does the ancient Stoic metaphysics stack up against modern scientific theories?

The Stoic approach is first and foremost a 'statistical' one. Looking to the wisdom of the ages (the musings of wise people across different eras, nations and cultures) the Stoic asks, what is the common ground (the 'common perceptions') to be found across the millennia? From east to west the issue of how the material world came to be as it is has been discussed in great depth. And there are two 'ideas' that come to light.

One. While everything in existence appears to have a 'birth' and a 'death', in actual fact there is a continuum whereby everything evolves or grows from what was already there. The various religions and wise people were right when they saw that there was a process of 'creation' as far as our planet is concerned. In fact, cosmologists have been able to offer a very good explanation of the processes involved in the formation of stars and planets in that they are observing areas in deep space where gravity is taking vast clouds of 'space dust' and is giving birth to new stars in the same manner as our solar system was originally 'created'.

But none of this supports the idea of a planet, let alone the whole Universe, being created out of nothing. The wise recognise that 'God' is an engineer and is not a magician.

If one comes across a creation theory that has a 'beginning' one is always left with the question, "What was there before that beginning?" The answer has to be that the totality of what exists is the same totality that has always been, only its form changes – a principle that Einstein and others have confirmed.

So we may conclude that the Cosmos is eternal and it rejuvenates itself through its own self destruction – not through a 'big bang' or a 'Cosmos-wide conflagration' and then start all over again from scratch; but through the growth and death of the individualised parts within itself. While the material that makes up Planet Earth will have gone through many 'conflagrations', as was to some degree envisaged by the Stoics of old, we now know that the Cosmos does not need to be totally 'destroyed' and/or recreated in order to explain its existence. Scientists describe us individuals, Mother Earth and our whole solar system as being made out of 'star dust' that comes from previous stars and planets that have died – there is no knowing how many times this process of solar death and rebirth has happened. What the Stoics of old described as 'regular conflagrations' where our planet is totally destroyed can now be seen as our solar system being engulfed in flames when our sun eventually explodes – just as the scientists have told us is liable to be the outcome for Mother Earth.

And when it comes to the cycles of solar creations and destruction, we are told that the creation of many of the chemical elements and subatomic particles can be attributed to the processes that happen within stars and the processes that occur during the death of the stars. So the idea that such elements were created as a result of the 'big bang' that supposedly created the whole Cosmos is unnecessary. By applying 'Occam's Razor' we can see that to explain what the scientists have discovered, there is no need for any theory that suggests that the Cosmos has a beginning.

Some scientists offer us a more cogent view of the science of existence, the rationale of which shows that, at the larger scale of the Cosmos, it is not necessary for the Cosmos to have an absolute beginning. It is more logical to accept that the Cosmos has always existed as an ever-changing state of Existence. It is also logical to accept that while our solar system has a finite lifespan, that the part of the Cosmos that scientists perceive of as the 'observable expanding universe' may be eternal. At this scale of existence all we have are theories, theories about the creation and the end of the Universe.

While science still looks to theories predicting the death of the Universe, it is near to giving up on its early creation story, the 'Big Bang Theory', and is having to look to try to understand what existed before the 'expanding universe' started to expand. And the answer to this is to be found in the Stoic metaphysics and the second 'common perception'.

Two. The second 'idea' that comes to light is the principle that there has to be some form of 'consciousness' that 'causes' the whole of existence to be as it is – be it called the Divine Fire, God, the Tao, or whatever. Or as was written of the early Stoic view:

"That right reason that pervades everything, being the same with Jupiter [God], who is the regulator and chief manager of all existing things."
Diogenes Laertius LIII

Diogenes goes on to say of the Stoic metaphysics:

*"There are two general principles in the universe, the active
and the passive. That the passive is matter, an existence
without any distinctive quality. That the active is the reason
which exists in the passive, that is to say God. For that he
being eternal, and existing throughout all matter, makes
everything."*
Volume LXVIII

These two 'principles', the passive and the active, are described as
being indivisible – they simply describe two qualities of the same
Oneness. To the Stoic way of seeing things, matter and consciousness
are two facets of the one state of being.

And science is moving towards the same conclusion where, in order to
explain many aspects of science, but more especially that of the
quantum world, scientists have to talk of 'consciousness' – or indeed
'The Consciousness' as some scientists call it.

From Sir James Jeans (1877 – 1946, an English physicist and
astronomer) we have the following quotes:

*"The stream of human knowledge is heading towards a non-
mechanical reality. The universe begins to look more like a
great thought than a great machine. Mind no longer appears
to be an accidental intruder into the realm of matter. We are
beginning to suspect that we ought rather to hail it as the
creator and governor of this realm."*
His book The Mysterious Universe (1930), p. 137.

He is also reported as saying

*"I incline to the idealistic theory that consciousness is
fundamental, and that the material universe is derivative from*

*consciousness, not consciousness from the material universe...
In general the universe seems to me to be nearer to a great
thought than to a great machine. It may well be, it seems to
me, that each individual consciousness ought to be compared
to a brain-cell in a universal mind."*

And

*"What remains is in any case very different from the full-
blooded matter and the forbidding materialism of the
Victorian scientist. His objective and material universe is
proved to consist of little more than constructs of our own
minds. .... Mind and matter, if not proved to be of similar
nature, are at least found to be ingredients of one single
system."*

And while Sir James clearly offers a less materialistic view than that of
the ancient Stoic teachings, from professors Brian Cox and Jeff
Forshaw ['The Quantum Universe: everything that can happen does
happen.' 2011 Penguin Books] we have the claims that subatomic
particles can be in more than one place at a time and that they 'explore'
the whole Universe when they move their location. We are also told
that as a result, being made up out of particles, a ball also 'knows' which
trajectory to follow when it is thrown because it too 'explores' every
possible path within the Universe.

We are also told that when an electron, proton or neutron in an atom
'settles into a particular state' it already has 'knowledge' of the state of
every other electron, proton or neutron in the Universe. Cox and
Forshaw describe this as 'an intimacy between the particles that make
up our Universe that extends across the entire Universe.'

These two professors, in keeping with many others, find a need to talk of aspects of consciousness and purpose when trying to describe what they believe is going on – they talk of 'exploring', 'knowing', 'knowledge' and 'intimacy'. However, despite the rationale of their ideas leading us to a 'recognition' of some form of consciousness, their ideas are sometimes irrational for they are still trying to find 'solutions' at the smallest of levels. For an individual particle to 'know' what every other similar particle in the Universe is doing it would need a brain the size of the Universe. The claim that there is "an intimacy between the particles that make up our Universe that extends across the entire Universe", is closer to what is a rational conclusion.

Science is now having to talk of 'fields' that extend throughout the Universe, fields that impart 'qualities' to particles and/or make particles "pop in and out of existence". There is but a small 'leap of faith' from acceptance that there is some form of unified Field of Consciousness that permeates the whole Cosmos and causes the Cosmos to manifest as it does to the acceptance of the Stoic metaphysics.

Science is effectively looking at the Consciousness that causes each subatomic particle to 'pop into existence' from a state of non-existence – that is a sea of possibility – and that acts as a coordinating 'master program' that imparts what 'knowledge' each subatomic particle needs in order to exist and to coordinate with the rest of Universe. No longer does the particle need to 'explore' the whole Universe instantaneously at every moment in order to 'know' about the state of every other similar particle. It is instead reasonable, and certainly more rational, to assume that each particle is manifested by, and is part of, the overall Consciousness that permeates the Cosmos and which imparts to the particle all the 'Information' that it needs in order to exist as it does.

Science is looking ever further into the subatomic world to try to find the 'first principles' that make up the subatomic particles and forces etcetera while also looking outwards to see when the Universe was

'Created' in order to try to explain what they see. They are looking to discover how 'matter' is constructed and to try to understand the creation, history and evolution of our part of the Cosmos – the 'observable Universe' or the 'expanding Universe'.

They are examining and theorising about Existence as they find it through observation and experimentation. That is fine in order to try to advance knowledge, but it is sufficient for the Stoic way of life to simply know that science has not negated the Stoic view of the Cosmos as a conscious living singular state of being. It is sufficient, at present, to know that science appears to be moving towards confirming the Stoic take on matters rather than denying it.

As the prime principle to which all other Stoic principles and ideas are referenced back to, Stoicism tells us that every 'thing' within the Cosmos is an individualised aspect of the singular living conscious Cosmos. We as 'individuals' are part of "this one living being" - we are 'sparks of the singular sea of mind-matter that manifests the whole of existence'.

We are manifested out of the body of the Cosmos and so we are one with the Cosmos. In Stoicism this may equally be stated as, "We are manifested out of the body of God and so we are one with God." As such we come to another of the Stoic principles - any harm we do to the whole we do to ourselves for we are one with the whole. This naturally leads on to another Stoic principle – as individuals, for our own sakes, we are guided to try to live in a manner that is as harmonious and in keeping with the nature of the life we have been born into as we are able.

And every other aspect of the search for the understanding as to how the art of living life is to be achieved is predicated on this one thought – the Cosmos is a living conscious state of being. The Cosmos is the body of God.

To repeat the words of Marcus Aurelius:

"Constantly regard the universe as one living being, having one substance and one soul; and observe how all things have reference to one perception, the perception of this one living being; and how all things act with one movement; and how all things are the cooperating causes of all things that exist; observe too the continuous spinning of the thread and the structure of the web."

The Manifestation of All That Is – a rationalisation

The Stoics "think that there are two general principles in the universe, the active and the passive. That the passive is matter, an existence without any distinctive quality. That the active is the reason which exists in the passive."
Diogenes Laertius LXVIII

In accord with Zeno's methodology, if we do not in the least have a framework of knowledge about the physical nature of Existence, and hence our place within it, how can we possibly know how to live life.

And one thing that Zeno was certain of is that the whole of Existence, together with everything that happens or exists within it, is physically real. But how is this physical state of existence manifested? The answer to this question helps to put the whole of life into context.

Zeno saw the four elements and the whole of physical existence as being manifested out of a finer 'creative material' that is both 'solid' and 'conscious' at the same time.

This turned out to be a remarkable insight.

Today, from an overview of much of the advances in knowledge, it may be seen that all that we experience is manifested as it is through the interplay of three 'primary dimensions' rather than four – and these three 'primary dimensions' are Space, Movement and Consciousness.

What are commonly called the 'three dimensions' are simply 'secondary dimensions' and are aspects and measurements of volume. It is also clear that volume, as we know it here on Planet Earth, is just one aspect of a complex multi layered interrelating system of measurement and location needed to fully identify a 'three dimensional' object in space.

In Zeno's time, Planet Earth was seen as being stationary with the heavens circulating around it, so any given volume was effectively seen to occupy one place in space relative to the surface of the planet. However, we now know that volumes exist within volumes and volumes also move within volumes. One can use the normal 'three dimensions' to describe a simple volume from a particular perspective, but if one tried to track that volume one would have to refer to many other levels of volume and movement.

Consider a box here on Earth – it is what we call 'three dimensional' and so it has a volume, but that volume is moving in Space as the planet spins and so exists within the rotating volume that is the biosphere of the planet, and the planet and its biosphere as a single volume is moving within the volume that is the solar system, and so on. Eventually one arrives at the volume that is the 'visible Universe' as seen by scientists.

Even though scientists often do not 'recognise' a further level of volume because they have no way of identifying it, there has to be at least one other level of volume into which the 'expanding Universe' is expanding (assuming that it really is expanding) – especially if the scientists are right about the nature of the Universe as they see it. How many more levels of 'background' volume are there that we will never know about?

What we do know, is that volumes as we experience them are individualised aspects of Space.

The Cosmos is 'the whole and the all', seen as the ultimate system that contains and coordinates all other individualised systems. It has a base requirement of needing a property that allows individualities within it to have volume so that they can exist in relationship to each other. The Stoics of old talked of this property as an 'extension'. This property is the 'primary dimension' Space. The dimension Space is a base requirement if the Cosmos is to manifest as it does.

Space manifests relativity.

Space is the stage on/in which the play of life is acted out. And it is no coincidence that the Stoics of old used the concept of a play being acted out on a stage as a metaphor for life itself.

The second base requirement for the manifestation of the Cosmos is Movement. We now know that every aspect of material existence is moving and interacting. The scientists have shown this from their study of cosmology on down to the study of the subatomic world - from the largest to the smallest, Movement is seen to be an inherent feature of everything that exists. It may even be said that Movement is what the ancient Stoics recognised as being 'the passive principle' in 'matter'. Movement in its many manifested forms may also be referred to in more scientific terms as 'energy'.

Science tells us that, even in deepest space, at every point, movement is to be found, including particles 'popping in and out of existence'. At a point, scientific study sees subatomic particles as little more than 'waves.' All sense of 'fixed stationary solidity' vanishing as one looks ever closer to the limits of our ability to observe the subatomic world. Even forces such as gravity may be seen as aspects of Movement.

But this primary dimension called Movement takes on an even wider meaning when talking of the nature of the Cosmos from Zeno's point of view, for it is 'the flow of change in the Experiential Moment'. It is this Movement that we experience as physical existence. If there is no Movement, there will be no Existence. Stillness does not exist anywhere in the Cosmos – not even in the most isolated area of Space.

Movement is not just the physical movement of an object from one place to another. It is the very means whereby existence can be manifested within Space. The dimension Movement is the potential to manifest any given state of existence at any given point within Space as required.

The whole Cosmos only exists here and now, in the same moment that we as individuals are experiencing the 'here and now', and it is within this Experiential Moment that change happens. (It is to be noted that the word 'moment' that relates to what we see as 'time' has the same root meaning as the word 'movement'.) We are not talking about the 'history' of change and evolution that is our memory of what was and how it became what it is now, but rather the active flow of change as it is happening now. And 'active', 'change' and 'movement' are all different words for describing the same aspect of the state of being that is the Cosmos.

Movement is the 'mechanism' that enables the ongoing manifestation of existence within Space, together with all the individual states to be found within it.

The primary dimensions of Space and Movement are the means whereby there is a potential for the physical Cosmos, as we know it, to be manifested as it is - just as a television offers the potential for programs to be displayed. A television has a screen and the means to show action pictures, but none of the pictures would happen without the input of the signal from the broadcaster that takes the potential of the television to show pictures on to the actuality of the television showing the program.

And this is where the primary dimension Consciousness comes in. It is the third base requirement for the manifestation of Existence.

Science shows that there are laws of science and laws of nature – 'permanent' rational processes that enable things to be as they are. Science is also beginning to see that the very processes that happen at the subatomic level and the quantum level need the involvement of some form of 'Consciousness' in order to explain 'how things work'.

We are told that quantum mechanics is fundamentally the ability to describe reality in the form of waves and 'probability'. And 'something' is needed to translate what is 'a sea of waves of probability' into the synchronised physical Universe that we experience.

We have moved on from our part of the Cosmos being seen by some scientists in the 20th century as 'an accidental blip of organisation in a sea of chaos' to seeing that everything manifests as it does as a result of the input of 'Information'. And 'Information' suggests some form of organising system that creates order.

Scientists have claimed such things as, "for the Universe to exist there had to be an observer" (their error being in the use of the past tense) and that "every particle in the Universe has to be 'aware' of the state of every other similar particle in the Universe".

The only rational explanation for such ideas is the existence of some form of 'self-observing Consciousness' that imparts 'information' instantaneously to all parts of the Cosmos (instantaneously rather than at the speed of light). As the Stoics of old called it, "the universal governor and manager of all things".

People who play games on computers would recognise it as akin to the master program that sets up the boundaries and the rules of the game that enables the game to be played. With the computer game, the 'master program' is that which enables the game to be manifested on the screen (Space) and is that which provides the means for the game to proceed (organised and purposeful Movement). The master program sets up and controls the progress of the game through various subprograms while allowing the gamer to play and affect the course of the game.

The master program controls much of the 'background' to the game (the laws of science and nature). The master program is that which causes the game to be as it is and to appear on the screen and as such the master program is not part of the game. However, the master program, through its various subprograms, is involved in the progress of the game and so adapts the game to the input of the gamer and allows the gamer to influence the outcome of the game - for good or for bad.

So also, the primary dimension Consciousness is not strictly part of the play of life, for it is the play of life. In a way, it is not part of Existence for it is that which enables Existence to be manifested as the rational coherent state that it is. However, it is also to be found permeating the whole Cosmos ready to adapt the play of life to the input of the 'will' of the many 'conscious' individualisations within the Cosmos.

The primary dimensions of Space, Movement and Consciousness as described are a conceptual framework for understanding different aspects of the 'singular coordinating system' that manifests all that exists. It is through an understanding of the interconnectedness of all three of these 'primary dimensions' that we can have some visualisation/concept as to how the Cosmos is made to manifest as it does.

We may not know exactly what the 'primary dimensions' of Space, Movement and Consciousness are or how they work, for that would require that we be able to see even further 'behind the scenes' of Existence. However, we can be aware of how they impinge on Existence, despite the fact that there will always be a limit beyond which science will not be able to go.

Over two thousand three hundred years ago Plato reported that Socrates said, "The Universe has plenty of Limit, an equal amount of Unlimit, and also a potent Cause which brings order and arrangement" and these ideas may be directly translated as the primary dimensions of Space, Movement and Consciousness. The dimension Space gives us the quality of 'Limit'. Movement, through the infinite possibilities it offers us, gives us the quality 'Unlimit'. And Consciousness, seen as God, offers us the 'potent Cause'.

And as stated, the Stoics of old talked of two indivisible principles that can be seen in the Cosmos - the passive principle as being matter without form, and the active principle as being the 'reason' that pervades all of existence so transforming the passive into the many aspects of the Cosmos that we know of around us – that is, Movement and Consciousness, with Space being described as a sort of 'extension'.

In this respect, these thinkers were not considering how the Universe evolved to become what it is. They were instead looking to how the Universe is 'manifested' here and now.

Zeno and his Stoics arrived at their ideas based on their study of the 'common perceptions' of the day, drawing from all the philosophies they came across – the philosophies of Greece as well as the philosophies from East to West and from North to South - whereby they concluded that, for Existence to exist there has to be a 'oneness of purpose' and a 'principle' that ensures that the Cosmos exists in harmony with itself – a 'consciousness' that they described as "the universal governor and manager of all things".

Despite all the destructive and creative forces that are to be found throughout the Cosmos, it still exists as a coordinated whole. So it is seen to be reasonable to see the Cosmos as a single entity that is manifested by a single coordinating Consciousness.

Science has an issue regards the nature of 'consciousness' and how it can have evolved out of a supposed strictly physical unconscious mechanical happening that their cosmic picture has painted in the past. For Stoicism there is no such issue, for 'Consciousness' is an intrinsic aspect of the physical Existence and as such it did not need to 'evolve' out of anything for it has always been there as an aspect of the very nature of Existence as a whole.

Consciousness offers a counterbalance to entropy.

Science is gradually coming to the same conclusions and is developing ideas about the interconnectedness of all aspects of the Cosmos, even down to the instantaneous coordination of subatomic particles – no matter how far apart they are. In order to arrive at a complete understanding of the nature of the Cosmos and how it is manifested, through their theorising about such things as the 'Higgs Field', science is demonstrating the need for some form of "universal governor and manager of all things" that permeates the whole Cosmos and that coordinates matters instantaneously throughout every corner of the Universe.

And recognising this interconnectedness of all that exists through 'the single conscious state that permeates the whole Cosmos' colours how the Stoic starts to view all that is around them and how at many levels such knowledge will impinge on their view of their place in Existence – for, at a personal level, the group of particles that manifest as our individual physical bodies contains a 'spark' of the Consciousness of the whole Cosmos – 'God is within us'.

At the very least, through the particles that form our bodies, we are inextricably one with the whole Cosmos. Albeit, that we may be seen to be insignificant when compared with the vastness of the Cosmos as we now know it, it is to be seen that we do have an effect on the state of the Cosmos in our neck of the woods - for we and it are one.

Just look at our effect as a species on the balances within the biosphere that is our mother planet. What we do in our individual lives needs to be considered against what we do as part of the human race and the effect of our species on the Whole.

An Alternate History of Time and the Experiential Moment

From a collection of writings regards the Stoic view on time we have:

SVF II 571 *Time is the interval of the world's motion and movement*

SVF II 514 *Most of the Stoics assert that motion itself is the essence of time.*

SVF II 518 *Chrysippus says that 'past and future time are non-existent, but have subsisted (or will subsist); only present time exists.*

An understanding of the nature of 'time' is fundamental to understanding our relationship to the whole of Existence.

In order to carry out their observations and calculations scientists have a need to view 'time' in a particular way. Unfortunately, this can lead to theorising that goes down blind alleys in that many people talk as if 'time' actually exists as a physical state and, together with many science fiction writers, believe that we are 'travelling through time' in a similar manner to how we travel through 'space'. In fact, they go so far as to combine 'space' and 'time' into a single theoretical state of 'space-time'.

However, as claimed by the Stoics of old, 'time' of itself does not exist.

In many respects, 'time' is nothing more than a system of measurement and as such it is not that which it measures.

'Time' is a means of mentally ordering and physically measuring our experience of Existence as a flow of change. 'Time' is the means to understand this flow of change and to be able to use experience of the flow of change to have some idea as to what to expect from the ongoing flow of change that is Existence.

So we have 'time' as our experience of the flow of change that is a core aspect of the nature of Existence – a means of mentally ordering events, etcetera. And we have what now may be described as 'clock time' whereby we measure the relationship between past states of existence, the present state of existence and possible future states of existence whereby we consider matters relative to a specific stage in the changing 'experiential moment' – more about the 'experiential moment' a little later.

'Clock time' for us originated as the human experience of the cycle of day and night, the changing of the seasons and the like.

We started to standardise such into measurement systems – most probably starting with crude sundials.

Once we had established a measurement for the length of a day by observing the movement of the sun in the sky we went on to observe the length of a year, lunar cycles and many other observations of regular cycles of natural events and over the years we have standardised these into weeks, months and years.

As we 'progressed' we found the need to be able to break the day down into measurable segments, but there was an issue in that we could not measure 'the passing of time' very efficiently when we could not see the sun. At first this was done by crude timers such as where some substance was allowed to seep from a container whereby it would take from noon on one day to noon on the next day to empty the container or through burning a candle that was designed to burn for a day. Through such instruments it was possible to set markers on the measuring instrument that would indicate how much 'time had passed' – and so eventually we came to the concept of 'the hours of the day'.

With more progress, the concepts of minutes and seconds were developed so that we could measure 'the passing of time' ever more accurately – and in the end we came up with clocks and watches as measuring instruments. To the point whereby we now have fantastically accurate clocks that use regular repeating subatomic events as a standard for the measurement of a 'second of time'.

Scientists have now defined 'one second' as 'the period it takes for one caesium electron to oscillate exactly 9,192,631,770 times.' And so, instead of taking the cycle of the sun as the standard for measuring 'the passing of time', we take our new 'standardised second' and multiply it up to arrive at one minute, one hour, one day and one year etcetera.

OK, we have to make some adjustments to our now standard system of measurement in order to keep these super accurate clocks in line with what actually goes on in the real world – such as having to adjust the measurement of the passing of years by adding in a leap day (29th February) every four years. All of which confirms that, despite setting up a highly accurate measurement system through 'clock time', in fact our measuring systems do not accurately reflect reality as we experience it in everyday life.

And here we come to the difference between 'clock time' and 'the passing of time'.

Scientists and science fiction writers can theorise about 'travelling through time' – including traveling back in 'time' – but as 'time' does not exist except in our minds or as a measuring system, it is not possible to travel 'through' it.

Time is not a 'prime dimension'.

To understand the relevance of 'time' we need to understand what it is measuring.

As we are told in the Fragments quoted above, time is the experience of, or the measurement of change.

So to understand 'time' we need to understand the nature of change.

If one travels from A to B and back from B to A one does not arrive at the same 'place' as one started out from, let alone at the same 'time'. When one arrives back at A one certainly is not back at the same 'moment' that one left A. One is also 'somewhere else' for 'point A' has also been travelling through space as a result of change going on all around.

If one travels from Delhi to Mexico City and then returns to Delhi one has not returned to exactly the same place in space as one set out from for the World has moved round its axis and the World has moved in relation to its orbit around the Sun and so on. So many processes of change whereby, in truth, Delhi is constantly moving in space albeit that in relation to its place on the surface of the planet Delhi is apparently to be found only in one place. Also, by the very nature of the constant change that has gone on in Delhi, the Delhi one returns to is not exactly the same Delhi as it was when one left it. Babies have been born. People have died. Building projects have progressed. Other buildings have deteriorated.

So while Delhi has moved within space, it has also undergone change and it is this overall flow of change that we casually talk of as 'time passing' when in fact we are talking about what is an active flow of change and, instead of science talking of 'the arrow of time', it is more correct to talk of 'the arrow of change' in that change cannot be reversed. All that one can do is to make new changes that brings one to an approximation of the situation prior to the initial change. But despite such attempts to recreate an earlier state, what is recreated will never be the same as the original state in that the original state no longer exists as it will be part of the memory that is the 'past'. The original state will have ceased to be part of Existence.

In relation to 'Past', 'Present' and 'Future' we do not travel from the Past, into the Present and on into the Future.

What is Past is past and it cannot be changed for there is no active process in the Past. And as such the Past no longer 'exists' other than as a 'memory'. The Past and Future do not exist other than as concepts to enable us to learn from experience and to forecast the probable state of events as they are liable to unfold.

All that we perceive as being 'the Future' is simply possibilities of what may happen as a result of the flow of change that is occurring now (in the Experiential Moment) combined with what may occur as a result of what is being consciously 'determined' in the Experiential Moment.

Some aspects of what we see as 'the Future' seem almost a certainty because of the mechanics of 'cause and effect' and the Laws of Nature. But it is to be remembered that scientific ideas about 'cause and effect' expressly exclude the intervention of any 'outside' action when trying to predict how a 'closed' mechanical system will progress. But as Consciousness permeates the Cosmos, no system is purely mechanical and so 'cause and effect' is not all powerful.

Simply because of the conscious actions of us humans, and other 'living' individuals, the Future is not fully 'preordained' – the idea that the Future is pre-determined is based on an assumed belief that the Cosmos is a mechanical system only. However, all living conscious beings add to the unknowability of what is to be. And when it comes to the Consciousness that is an aspect of how the Cosmos is manifested, we can have no knowledge as to what influence this may have regards shaping the flow of change – the whole future is up for grabs. It is simply a matter of probability.

We are in fact all living in a state of change and change only happens in 'the here and now.' Only the Present moment exists in that Existence is manifested out of the active process of change and such change is the process of manifesting the Cosmos through Movement and this only happens in 'the here and now' – the Experiential Moment. What we call the 'Present' or the 'now' is where Existence exists. It is where the Cosmos is made manifest.

The whole of the Cosmos exists and always has existed only in the Experiential Moment. Everything only exists in 'the Now'. We do not move along in a flow of time. We stay in the one Experiential Moment and experience the flow of change around us and within us as it happens.

All change happens simultaneously. All 'events' as they are manifested across the Universe in the Experiential Moment occur simultaneously. Observation of the flow of change has a problem with what may be considered as simultaneousness, but such is only a problem regards the process of observation. It is not a problem with the reality that everything is part of a simultaneous active flow of change that is occurring from one side of the Universe to the other.

Time, seen as the 'rate' of the flow of change, is a constant across the whole Universe regardless of any distance or relative motion.

Once change occurs because of the flow of change, the state of the Cosmos as it was ceases to be – all that exists from the 'Past' is a memory in the 'now'.

The fossilised dinosaur bones exist now, and through them we have a 'memory' of what they were probably like in an earlier state of the Experiential Moment when the dinosaur was alive.

As light from a distant star arrives here on Earth for some astronomer to view it, all they are viewing is the light here on Earth – they are not viewing the star as it is 'now' – they are viewing a 'memory' of a star as it existed years ago, the memory being kept alive by the light it emitted during an earlier state of the Experiential Moment. For all the astronomer knows, the star may no longer exist at this stage in the Experiential Moment. The light we see has travelled to here as a result of the flow of change and as such has always existed within the Experiential Moment, just the position of the light within Space has altered.

To say it again, Existence is the active flow of change and there is no active flow of change in what we call 'the Past'. All that is to be experienced can only be experienced in the Now.

Such theoretical ideas as 'multiple time-lines' that suggest that every possibility actually happens so causing every possible 'Future' to happen are totally irrational – such is the makings of science fiction. Such are not rational nor are they reasonable beliefs.

There is only one Experiential Moment and it is here that the 'happening' that is Existence happens. There are no 'parallel Universes'. There is only one – and it is the Cosmos in which we exist.

What is 'Past' is fixed for it 'has happened' and so cannot be changed. We cannot change the Past.

What is seen as the 'Future', being a 'forecast of a possibility' or 'probability', can be changed. We can try, in the present moment, to move the flow of change in a different direction than it would normally go if left solely to the mechanics of 'cause and effect'. How successful our individual attempts to affect the flow of change, so as to bring into reality a hoped-for future state of the Present, is a whole other question.

Within the Experiential Moment we are faced with what cannot be changed because, as a result of the flow of change, it is now the Past. What we are faced with is 'as good as it gets'. All the wishing things could be other than what they are is fruitless. The 'immediate Past' is where the flow of change has brought us to. It is fixed, for the active flow of change is moving on. But as the active flow of change moves on, we are also faced with how we can influence the probability of a particular Future through understanding what can be changed in the Experiential Moment – how we can influence the 'flow of change' in the hope of leading to a better 'future' Present.

The 'Present' is not the sudden 'flat' interface between Past and Future – it is an event, or more correctly 'the constant ongoing event that is the Cosmos being made manifest'.

Some present scientific theories that have such things as subatomic particles traveling back in time are clearly based on incorrect visualisation as to what 'time' really is. By understanding 'time' as the flow of change within the Experiential Moment we can see that Space/Time as used by many scientists ought to be seen more correctly as Space/Change. Such would eliminate the false ideas as to anything being able to travel back in time.

We can only 'travel in time' by staying within the Experiential Moment and so experience 'the passing of time'.

So, as Zeno tells us, it becomes clear that what we do with the life we have been given is what counts. We can be the bit-part actor in the play of life that offers nothing more than to make up the numbers, or we can learn to be the skilful actor whose life contributes to the betterment of the play overall, regardless of our role within the play.

Within limits, we are free to try to help determine how the flow of change will progress within our neck of the woods. As there are so many other factors determining the direction of the overall flow of change, what we try to determine may not always come to fruition. But if we do not at least try we will never be able to play our part in determining what happens next.

We can be 'puppets' or 'robots'. Or we can be 'skilful actors' or 'gamers' helping to develop the flow of the play of life.

At the same time, such an understanding of the nature of the Past, Present and Future will help us to be more accepting of what we cannot change and so more accepting of what is.

6. How Zeno's Stoicism is still relevant today

"Stoicism is "one of the loftiest and most sublime philosophies in the record of Western civilization. In urging participation in the affairs of man, Stoics have always believed that the goal of all inquiry is to provide man with a mode of conduct characterised by tranquillity of mind and certainty of moral worth." And "the themes of universal brotherhood and the benevolence of divine nature makes Stoicism one of the most appealing of philosophies."
[Encyclopaedia Britannica; 'Stoicism. Philosophical Schools & Doctrines.' Copyright 2004. Used with permission]

Stoicism is both a philosophy of life and a religion. In Zeno's time the word 'philosophy' meant 'the love of wisdom' and, in this context, the word 'religion' carries no more intent other than the claim that Stoicism involves an element of 'faith' supported by the wise use of knowledge. We are not talking of some academic branch of 'philosophy' as taught in universities nor of 'organised religion' with all of the trappings that come with such.

Stoicism does not involve accepting anything on faith alone. Zeno and his fellow Stoics, like Socrates before them, questioned everything, and the would-be Stoic is encouraged to do likewise.

So, to setting Stoicism in its historical context. From Socrates to Zeno and beyond, the great Athenian schools of thought were faced with a populous that suffered all manner of psychological problems resulting from the nature of 'civilisation' at the time. The constant warring, the constant power struggles amongst the elite and the constant threat to the individual's security of family, property and life left many in heightened states of emotion and a reduced ability to view life rationally. One unguarded comment at the wrong time or one individual trying to curry favour with someone in power by telling tales (true or false) could throw one's life into chaos. On top of this, the stability that the religions of the day had offered was gradually being eroded. The framework of beliefs on which people based their lives was gradually being broken down.

(Sounds sort of familiar. Nothing much has changed even up to today.)

Despite being immersed in such a society, the thinkers of the ancient Athenian schools tried to find a new framework by which to live, while also looking to 'cure' the epidemic of mental illness.

Unfortunately, the thinkers were a product of their age and as a result they were often blinded to the very wisdom they were trying to develop. Just as today, many of the thinkers tried being over intellectual in their approach to the problems and so went down blind alleys, often seeking after 'the ideal'. Theirs was an elitist society and this is reflected in the many attempts to work out how the 'ideal' society would govern itself. And of course, the various schools had their imagined 'ideal' societies being governed by 'ideal' people – 'sages'.

While we are told that Zeno also looked to how society could be better managed, probably falling into the same trap as the founders of the other schools, Zeno's approach to learning how to live is practical rather than being overly intellectual and idealised.

To this end, first and foremost Stoicism offers a framework of belief and practical observation that is centred in the principle that the nature of the Cosmos is that of a oneness that is 'a singular living rational being' of which we, as individuals, are a part.

Some may claim that this principle is 'blind faith', but today it is more based on two factors. The one is the ancient wisdom that there exists 'a friend beyond phenomena' ['Stoics and sceptics' 1913, Edwyn R

Bevan as referred to by Murray in his 1915 lecture] – that is a state of being that is known by many names by many different cultures but is to be seen as referring to a singular state that is common to all cultures over the ages. Within Stoicism many words are used to describe this 'friend' – God, the Logos, the divine spirit or fire, Nature (translated from the Greek word 'Phusis' which implies that Nature is living, evolutionary and rational) and many other such terms. In keeping with Zeno's rationale, the fact that such an idea is a 'common perception' of humankind gives it credence. It is part of the common wisdom of our species – the wisdom that says that all of this natural organisation we see about us has to have some Cause – a cause that is more than 'a blip of organisation in a sea of chaos'.

This is the second factor for accepting the Stoic beliefs in a deity. Pursuing knowledge through the study of the burgeoning natural sciences, in trying to understand the nature of the world in which they lived they looked around them and they saw organisation within the nature of the existence they experienced and so they reasoned that there had to be some 'thing' that coordinated this organisation. In speculating about how such an organising principle may operate within the physical world they talked about the 'finest of all matter out of which all other matter was manifested' – 'matter' where the passive principle and the active principle are to be seen as being irrevocably co-mingled or are to be seen as two qualities of the one 'substance' and where the active principle is a Consciousness that permeates the whole Cosmos.

While this belief in God as 'the universal governor and organiser of all things' was based on passed down wisdom and theories arrived at from simple observation, modern science has come up with the study needed to give support to the speculation.

What started out as a speculative assumption has today been given grounds to see such as a rational belief.

Stoicism believes that the Cosmos is to be seen as the body of God and that we exist within and as part of this body. God is perceived as being the 'mind' that permeates the whole physical Cosmos and as such is 'the universal governor and organiser of all things.' And in that we are a part of the body of God, so also the Stoic rationale tells us that we contain within our being 'a spark' of the 'mind of God'.

> *'We do not need to uplift our hands towards heaven… as if in this way our prayers were more likely to be heard. God is near you, he is with you, he is within you… The holy spirit indwells within us. One who marks our good deeds and our bad deeds, and is our guardian. Indeed, no man can be good without the help of God. … He it is that gives noble and upright counsel.'*
> Seneca XLI. On the God Within

A pretty powerful starting point for arriving at a framework of beliefs on which to base one's rationale regards how life works and that leads to a rationale as to how life ought to be lived.

There is much within the teachings of Stoicism that has commonality with other beliefs and philosophies. But key to understanding Stoicism as a whole and to living as a Stoic is the internalising of the Stoic belief in the nature of God and in accepting that we, as individuals, are the 'children of God' and that to live our lives well is to live our life in accord with the will of God.

> *"For I regard God's will as better than my will. I shall attach myself to Him as a servant and follower, my choice is one with His, my desire one with His, in a word my will is one with His will."*
> Epictetus IV.VII

Bearing this in mind, Stoicism seeks out how we ought to live.

What is your art? To be good. And how is this accomplished
well except by general principles, some about the nature of the
universe, and others about the proper constitution of man?
Marcus Aurelius XI.5

And here we are told that first and foremost the would-be Stoic wants
to be 'good' and that we can learn how to live as 'children of God' from
the knowledge that thrusts itself into our minds through our senses and
the knowledge that is the 'common perceptions or beliefs' of
humankind (seen as the ever-developing knowledge of humankind
together with the wisdom that has been passed down over the ages). If
we look at matters aright, the nature of the world about us tells us how
we ought to live so as not to be in conflict with the nature of Existence
as a whole or with our own nature as reasoning social animals. This is
the practical rather than intellectual approach that Stoicism offers us.

All of this is the core understandings from which Stoic ethics are
derived. The foundation of Stoic ethics is grounded in the recognition
of the oneness of all around us, in that all is manifested out of the body
of God and the subsequent realisation, that wherever we have influence
as individuals, that the good of the whole is what we ought to aim for.

'All things are mutually intertwined, and the tie is sacred, and
scarcely anything is alien the one to the other. For all things
have been ranged side by side, and together help to order one
ordered Universe. For there is both one Universe, made up of
all things, and one God immanent in all things, ... and one
Law, one Reason common to all intelligent creatures, and one
Truth.'
Marcus Aurelius VII.9

Just as it was in ancient Athens, still today through the Stoic rationale, it becomes obvious that each individual best serves themselves if they serve as many of the levels of society and Existence that they are part of as their circumstance will allow. Within Stoicism, care and concern for oneself is only considered as being what is needed in order to try to ensure that, as individuals, we can best serve the greater good.

But of course, as with any 'tool', if we are to best serve the whole, we need to ensure that we have been well 'honed'.

'The happy life... is a life that is in harmony with its own nature, and it can be attained in only one way. First of all, we must have a sound mind and one that is in constant possession of its sanity; second, it must be courageous and energetic, and, too, capable of the noblest fortitude, ready for every emergency, careful of the body and of all that concerns it, but without anxiety; lastly, it must be attentive to all the advantages that adorn life – the user, but not the slave, of the gifts of Fortune.'
Seneca 'On the Happy Life' iii

Note: In this context the word 'happy' is a misleading translation of the Greek word 'eudaimonia' which is more correctly translated as 'being possessed of good spirits'. 'Happy' has at its root the word 'hap' which relates to chance and so happiness is an emotional reaction to chance external events. Whereas for Stoicism 'being of good spirits' relates to a stable ongoing resilience and inner state of mind. Zeno described 'eudaimonia' as 'living in the smooth flow of life', and such may be better recognised as the state of being contented with 'what is' while still striving to partake in maintaining or improving the wellbeing of the whole as best as we are able.

In order to live a life in accord with the above, there is the need for the individual to be able to see reality for what it is, and this requires some degree of dispassionate observation and study. Such is an ongoing life discipline. Basically, the more appropriate knowledge a person has, the better will be their decisions as to how to live their individual lives in relationship to the whole.

In Stoicism, the ethics or morality of how to live is inseparable from the physical nature of Existence in that the ethics is arrived at by the logical and reasoned assessment of one's roles in the play of life in relationship to all else that is presented to us on the stage of life by way of 'scenery', 'props' and other 'actors'. The Stoic's aim is to learn from the life they find themselves in so as to be better able to 'adlib' as best as they can by developing their skill as an actor in that the play is not written in stone. The Playwright has offered us the means to discern the general direction they want the play to progress while leaving us the scope to use our skill as actors to help better progress the play as it is intended.

However, for the Stoic, God is still actively involved with us - in that God is an integral and ever-present part of the Existence in which we exist, and how the play works out will be better for Mother Earth, and so for us, if we work with God. It is better to work with Mother Nature than against her. And here 'Mother Nature' is a modern translation of the original Greek word Phusis where Phusis was seen in Stoicism as being another aspect of the living God.

This recognition of the oneness of all and that all is intertwined leads the Stoic to a rational assessment of how to live, with particular attention to the fact that 'rationale' has at its root the word 'ratio'. Living life well is a matter of wisely balancing all sorts of influences according to the ratio of their relevance while also being aware of the influence we can have.

It is obvious that, at present, beyond our planet we can have little influence. Where we can best apply our craft of living life well as individual Stoics is on our planet. Regardless of what influence our roles in life may allow us to have, by living the Stoic life we are more likely to influence matters for the good, even if it is only though living life in a manner that others will view as being the actions of a person of good character, whereby they may feel inclined to try to emulate our way of life and so help bring about the betterment of society as a whole.

We become Stoics, not to benefit ourselves, but to train ourselves to live in a manner whereby, given the opportunity, we will benefit those around us. And it is our belief in God and in the nature of the Cosmos as the body of God that provides the grounding that will help us to try to stick to our chosen path throughout our lives - come what may.

Stoicism is always about the greater good. We train to improve our practical wisdom in the hope that we may better understand how we need to act in order to be of help rather than a hindrance in such a project.

Unfortunately, together with the other schools of Athens, the Stoics of old got pulled into the question of 'the sage' – the perfectly wise person. The sage was not an invention of the Stoics. It was a technical intellectual standardised idea used in those days to discuss how 'the perfect person' would think and live if they followed this or that school's teachings. Together with other similar debating points the Stoics were expected to be able to provide answers to such issues. They found themselves trying to address the issue of 'the sage' in their writings, even though it was seen by Stoics that such ideas were often irrelevant in that the chasing after such an ideal is an impossibility.

Many in the Stoic community today argue that the 'ideal' that the concept of 'the sage' sets is needed to drive them on to seek to improve by offering them a target to aim for. And yet perversely they will also agree that sagehood is next to being an impossible state, if it is not a totally impossible state - in which case their target is little more than a mirage.

Not one of the Stoics of old, or anyone of the other schools, ever claimed to have achieved sagehood, so none were in a position to teach how to achieve such. In fact, Stoicism does not teach a path to sagehood. It teaches a path that the person in the street can follow that will make them a better person – that is, a person of greater benefit to all around them than they would have been without their Stoic training and beliefs.

'This is the mean of which I approve; our life should observe a happy medium between the ways of a sage and the ways of the world at large; all men should admire it, but they should understand it also.'
Seneca V. 'The Philosopher's Mean'

Not only should they understand it, but they must also be able to see that the Stoic life is achievable and has purpose.

Following the Stoic rationale, it is to be seen that Stoicism is lived moment by moment and that at any moment the Stoic may just manage to think, say and do just the right thing in accord with their knowledge and their correct use of that knowledge. This is what wisdom is and wisdom is the key character that the Stoic is trying to develop, where the four cardinal characters or virtues are just different aspects of the one character, namely wisdom. If you are acting wisely, you will be living up to all the other characters as needed.

The Stoic does not aim to become the sage. They instead aim, moment by moment, to live in accord with Nature, where such can be unpacked as:

Living moment by moment mindful of the Stoic beliefs and teachings, mindful of the individual Stoic's aim to learn how to live by looking to their examined knowledge of their own nature and their examined knowledge of the Nature of all around them – that is, their knowledge about the nature of life 'seen in all of its nakedness' - and mindful of their aim to fulfil all of their rolls in life to the benefit of society and of the Cosmos as best as their nature, abilities and circumstance will allow them.

Stoicism recognises that we are human. We will not get it right one hundred percent of the time.

We will not always be able to hold our concentration so as to be fully mindful at all times. What matters is how quickly our training will allow us to regain our mindful stance whereby, if our inattentiveness is leading us down inappropriate paths, our wisdom and our reason can lead us back to a path in harmony with Nature.

Our nature as animals is part of how we live and our instincts will lead us down paths that our reason has not had time to choose. What matters is how quickly we are able to bring to bear our training and beliefs so as to enable our reasoning faculty to confirm or correct the path our instincts have taken us on.

Our nature as animals will allow an unexamined feeling or impression to jump into our minds and possibly lead to involuntary, in the moment, reactions. What matters is how quickly we can bring our reasoning faculty to bear so as to recover from any initial reaction, such as the 'shock' that can be elicited by a loud unexpected noise.

In similar manner some inappropriate 'opinion' embedded deep inside of our mind may surface in reaction to some event, so leading to feelings that may swamp our reasoning faculty and so lead to actions that are not in accord with Nature. And this is at the heart of much of the Stoic training to achieve a sound mind – how to cleanse the mind of as many inappropriate 'opinions' as possible by looking to rationally examine them in light of our Stoic beliefs and cold reason, so being able to see the naked facts free from our 'emotional baggage'.

It is here that the Stoic can make most progress - by breaking down old inappropriate mind patterns and habituating a new Stoic mind-set that will allow the natural feelings of affection and the like to flourish while holding at bay the more violent, aggressive, feelings (perturbations) that will not answer to the rule of conscious reason, a reason that is looking to live in accord with Nature.

Habituation of ensuring the rule of conscious reason is what is behind much of the Stoic mind training, but such is of use to the bad person as much as to the wise person. What takes the Stoic training to the next level - that of aiming to be good - is the Stoic framework of beliefs in God and the nature of the Cosmos that form the grounding for how we see the world around us and our part within it.

Stoicism is not aiming for us to become the ideal sage. It is aiming for us to become a better human being – a being that is an animal that can be rational and reasoning and above all is a social animal by nature. It is not that we aim to 'make' the world a better place. It is that we 'try' to do so in the full knowledge that we cannot control the overall flow of change that is Existence, albeit that we may be able to bring some influence to bear whereby the flow of change may be all the better as a result of our input, or at the very least may hopefully be none the worse.

The Stoic aims to be part of the solution as against being part of the problem.

This does not require that we become the impossible 'ideal sage'. It just requires that we try our best as much as we possibly can - given our individual nature, our abilities and circumstance. Following Zeno's rationale tells us that living as a Stoic is an achievable aim, even today.

However, I have been careful to talk of following Zeno's rationale because such does not involve sticking to the sciences of his day or of tying ourselves down to ancient technical use of concepts that require that we are fully conversant with the ancient Greek language or its usage. Seneca tells us not to get too tied up in individual words but rather that we need to see the overall intent of what is being said.

Zeno's Stoicism tells us to follow Nature and as such Zeno's rationale is telling us that Stoicism needs to keep up with advancing knowledge about the nature of Existence. At the same time the rationale tells us to follow the 'common perceptions' of humankind – the wisdom passed down over the ages. Advancing knowledge ensures that we do not stagnate in a state of not investigating further, while the wisdom of the ages ensures that we do not jump on every bandwagon that claims to be providing improved knowledge.

So what we look to as Stoicism today needs to have its roots clearly in the Stoicism of old, especially regards those matters that do not change with time – such as our relationship to God. To drop such basic Stoic beliefs is to negate the whole of Stoicism.

But such does not stop us reworking some of the Stoic ideas so that they marry with advancing knowledge, such as the advances in cosmology and the like. Nor does it stop us from rewording some of the Stoic ideas in order to make such matters clear to the modern person. After all, there are many of the ancient Greek words that do not easily translate into our modern languages. In many cases we need to start from basics and rework the explanations and understandings while ensuring that we keep to the Stoic rationale that all of the Stoic teachings form a part of a singular whole that will enable the Stoic to know how to live life.

7. Control, Determinism and Providence according to the Stoic rationale

Every Stoic brings a piece of their own nature to their interpretation of the beliefs and principles of Stoicism, as is expected of a Stoic.

'This is what Zeno said. But what of your own opinion? This is the opinion of Cleanths. But what of your own opinion? How long shall you march under another man's orders. Put forth something of your own stock.'
Seneca XXXIII. On the futility of Learning Maxims

However, a Stoic's rationale is always grounded in the Stoic beliefs, metaphysics and principles.

'Meanwhile, I follow the guidance of Nature – a doctrine upon which all Stoics are agreed. Not to stray from Nature and to mould ourselves according to her law and pattern – this is true wisdom.'
Seneca On the Happy Life' iii

One arrives at a point where one agrees with this or else one does not and so does not go on to self-declare as being a Stoic.

Epictetus was a Stoic through and through. What we have of Epictetus' words, as reported by Arrian, covers a limited section of what he will have presented as the curriculum at his 'School for Sick Souls'. The teachings we have will have been grounded in the belief of the oneness of matter and mind – the passive and active principles of the prime matter that is the body of the Cosmos where the active principle is the God that Epictetus so wanted to align his will with. Epictetus will not have left such teachings out. Looked at properly it is to be seen that all that we do have of his teaching are predicated on the Stoic view of the Nature we are to align with.

The Stoic teachings as presented by Epictetus clearly connects Epictetus' views on control with Epictetus' belief in God.

But what says Zeus? "Epictetus, had it been possible I should have made both this paltry body and this small estate of thine free and unhampered. But as it is, let it not escape thee this body is not thine own, but only clay cunningly compounded.
Yet since I could not give thee this, we have given thee a certain portion of ourself, this faculty of choice and refusal, of desire and aversion, or, in a word, the faculty which makes use of external impressions; if thou care for this and place all that thou hast therein, thou shalt never be thwarted, never hampered, shalt not groan, shalt not blame, shalt not flatter any man. What then? Are these things small in thy sight?"
"Far be it from me!" "Art thou, then, content with them?" "I pray the Gods I may be."
Epictetus 'Of the things which are under our control and not under our control'

Prior to this piece Arrian quotes Epictetus as telling his students:

The same holds true of the art of music with regard to melodies; but whether you are at this moment to sing and play on the lyre, or neither sing nor play, it will not tell. What art or faculty, then, will tell? That one which contemplates both itself and everything else. And what is this? The reasoning faculty; for this is the only one we have inherited which will take knowledge both of itself - what it is, and of what it is capable, and how valuable a gift it is to us - and likewise of all the other faculties. For what else is it that tells us gold is beautiful? For the gold itself does not tell us. Clearly it is the faculty which makes use of external impressions. What else judges with discernment the art of music, the art of grammar, the other arts and faculties, passing judgement upon their uses and pointing out the seasonable occasions for their use? Nothing else does. As was fitting, therefore, the gods have put under our control only the most excellent faculty of all and that which dominates the rest, namely, the power to make correct use of external impressions, but all the others they have not put under our control.

Aligned with this, in the Encheiridion we are told:

Some things are under our control, while others are not under our control. Under our control are conception, choice, desire, aversion, and, in a word, everything that is our own doing; not under our control are our body, our property, reputation, office, and, in a word, everything that is not our own doing. Furthermore, the things under our control are by nature free, unhindered, and unimpeded; while the things not under our control are weak, servile, subject to hindrance, and not our own. Remember, therefore, that if what is naturally slavish you think to be free, and what is not your own to be your own, you will be hampered, will grieve, will be in turmoil, and will blame both gods and men; while if you think only what is your own to be your own, and what is not your own to be, as it really is, not your own, then no one will ever be able to exert compulsion upon you, no one will hinder you, you will blame no one, will find fault with no one, will do absolutely nothing against your will, you will have no personal enemy, no one

will harm you, for neither is there any harm that can touch you.
Epictetus The Encheiridion 1, 1 – 3

There are two things to consider when looking to how Epictetus presents matters. The one is that his views and terminology are coloured by his background as a slave whereby 'control' is equated to freedom in that freedom is a key aspect of his view of life. There is action that you are able to initiate yourself and follow through on, and then there is that over which others may use power or position to intervene and so take control and so force you along a path you would not initially have chosen. The story of the dog tied to the back of a horse and cart demonstrates that these two aspects can and often do overlap. Even the slave can bring to bear some influence on the outcome of many a situation.

The second thing is that Epictetus will have been well versed in the general Stoic view of the oneness of matter and mind. When looked at carefully his approach to training his students recognises this. Epictetus does not sell us a purely 'intellectual' approach regards the Stoic training methods. When Epictetus talks of 'everything that is our own doing' he is talking of 'choice' as being 'a physical action' perpetrated by both body and mind in that the Stoic physics, back to Zeno, tells us that body and mind are at the very least comingled to form a single state, if body and mind are not in fact two characters of the one state.

The rationale of Stoicism does not set up a dichotomy or a trichotomy of control. It simply tells us what we can gain and maintain a level of control over as a result of our possessing a free-will. It looks to what we are able to do as a result of having been gifted 'a spark of God' that manifests as the quality that makes us rational and reasoning animals and to what degree of 'influence' we can bring to bear on life as a result of us being only a 'spark of God'. We are looking at the reasoning faculty that enables us to make rational conscious choices that are the choices that combine an understanding of the need for acceptance of any limitations placed on us together with the ongoing drive that is the result of the 'correct use of external impressions' – in other words, 'the correct use of knowledge', which just happens to be a definition of 'wisdom'.

Within the Stoic world view such choices are physical actions. They do not just occur within our heads, but will be reflected in our internal bodily processes and our externally visible demeanour at the very least, and probably will lead to bodily actions that interact with the 'outer world'. These conscious choices/actions can, with the proper training, override our own inner programming as human animals whenever such is found to be necessary regards working towards our goals of developing a good character and of playing our part as citizens of the Cosmos.

Epictetus's teachings, as presented by Arrian, are in places a necessary simplification in that some of what he is offering is aimed at inducting young students who are at the beginning of their training into his school. Epictetus will have expected the students to eventually get to the point whereby the wider training in the Stoic rationale will have helped them to gain a better understanding of the many nuances that are to be found through a greater understanding as to how all the parts of Stoicism work together.

What is often missed today regards what we have from Epictetus is that we do not always have unhindered control over our 'reasoning faculty'.

Epictetus sets health as being outside of our full control and Seneca tells us that we need to be 'of sound mind' if we are to act as Stoics for it is recognised that at times the individual may lose the ability to be in control of their 'reasoning faculty' as a result of delirium or other sicknesses of the body or mind that lead to, at the very least, a temporary 'unsound mind' whereby their choices may be contrary to what they would have chosen had they been 'of sound mind'.

Within the Stoic rationale everything is subject to the overall 'networking' of the 'will' of the Cosmos and all that is within it, including our own will. There is no clear line between what is and what is not in our individual control.

Someone I have corresponded with has often claimed, as an example of 'a Stoic dichotomy of control', that he does not have control over his arm as his arm is an 'external' and so his use of his arm can be thwarted, whereas his choices are 'internal' and so cannot be thwarted.

And yet he was able to type emails using his arm in order to fulfil his choice to engage in debate with me. He was proving that he had control of his arm – at least until and unless some other aspect of the Cosmos hindered him. The reason he was able to use his arm was that he was acting 'in accord with Nature' and at the time nothing in the rest of Nature was hindering his choice to move his arm. 'To live in accord with Nature' is a call to act in accord with Nature – and Stoicism does not limit such action to only training oneself to think in accord with Nature. There is no living in accord with Nature unless one's thoughts AND actions are in accord with Nature.

So, as a result of our very nature as individuals there are matters over which, at times, we have total control within the limits of their nature, there are matters over which we can at times have partial control according to circumstance, and there are matters over which we have next to no control whatsoever except regards how we accept such matters for what they are. These are not a dichotomy or a trichotomy in that they are not opposed to each other.

The Stoics rationale leads us to think not of dichotomies but of matters 'ranged side by side' as parts of a singular Whole.

'For all things have been ranged side by side, and together help to order one ordered Universe.
Marcus Aurelius VII.9.

'Total control' and 'no control whatsoever' are misnomers, for degrees of control are just different aspects of a range of possibilities. They are part of a single spectrum and occur according to circumstance.

None of this negates the need for the Stoic to be aware at all times as to what degree they control their own inner state as well as to what degree they control external factors while also being aware as to how influences from external factors can control their lives – with or without their complicity. Without such awareness they will not be able to live their roles in life as they ought.

Epictetus may appear to concentrate on 'control' as being related to 'absolute freedom'. However, in the Stoicism that he is teaching, the 'control' that God has given us through gifting us a 'spark of God's own being' relates to how we aim to live our lives. And into this comes not just control, but the principle of acceptance and many other aspects that Stoicism teaches us.

For whatever reason, as we have been gifted a freewill, we are free to choose to 'live in accord with Nature' or not. However, if we are to live as Stoics and are to 'live in accord with Nature' we have to choose to surrender much of our personal 'freedom' and instead live for the common good.

Following the Stoic rationale regards 'control', it is to be seen that most people 'choose' through ignorance to be enslaved to what they incorrectly see as being of value in that they have not sought to be aware of the nature of the Cosmos and our relationship to it. Much of Epictetus' trainings that has survived to today relates to methods that are aimed at breaking this enslavement in order to help people regain 'a sound mind' together with sound judgements regards the 'value' of things – both regards us developing a good character and also as to what is of use for our fulfilling our roles in life. This training covers both the self-improvement and the service to society aspects of the Stoic life. Once the Stoic has freed their mind, their aim is to enter into service to the Cosmos by bringing their will into line with 'the will of God' - so living 'in accord with Nature'.

The Stoic seeks to free the control of their lives from 'the externals' that enslave them through ill perceived selfishness. And in parallel to this the Stoic surrenders their freedom to the selfless service of the Cosmos and society according to their circumstance, ability and nature.

And how does the Stoic know what it is to serve the Cosmos? By, as Epictetus tells us, making the 'correct use of external impressions'. Here we are back to the practical wisdom to be gained through observing the existence we are faced with. However, such 'living in accord with Nature' also involves us in attempting to align our actions with the Determinism and Providence that are properties attributed to God.

Through our link to God, we partake in the Determinism and Providence of God in that we can, with training and good health, have control over things that 'are of our doing'. And part 'of our doing' is to wisely contribute to fulfilling our part in determining how the flow of change will evolve for the betterment of all – that is, through acting with wise forethought.

Epictetus tells us:

'.... not under our control are our body, our property, reputation, office, and, in a word, everything that is not our own doing.'

Yet, to varying degrees of success or otherwise, in these matters we are able to have some influence. How much influence we have is dependent on other influences that affect our lives. Such things can be taken away from us by the course of Nature or they can be damaged by 'external' forces such as the actions of others etcetera.

It is the sudden loss of such matters, or the failure to achieve what we have aimed for where we only have the partial influence/control that Epictetus trains us to come to terms with. However, the societal side of the Stoic teachings would be groundless unless we choose to aim for what is good for society and that means that we must try to bring our influence to bear as is appropriate to our circumstance, ability and roles in life - even if we do not have 'total control'.

Just as the archer tries to control matters whereby their arrow will hopefully fly true, so we also try to control matters, even where we know we may not be able to keep total control over the situation. We direct our choices to initiate actions with the aim of seeing our chosen actions through to fruition, while being ready to have to accept any situation whereby the combination of what we have tried to influence together with the influence of any other outside force may lead to something we had not been aiming for.

Of course, life does not work as simply. Often debate about this area of Stoic teachings looks to individual events in isolation, whereas life is a flow whereby we are having to make a continuous stream of choices that are always adjusting to the flow of change.

So regardless of what control we have over events, our choices can influence the flow of life - be it that we have full control for a period of time over a small aspect of the Cosmos or only limited influence as to what happens regards our input. We are partaking in determining the forward flow of change in partnership with God and other individualities that have use of a 'spark' of the 'active principal'. We are part of God, the God that is the Cause that moves the flow of change within the experiential moment. As such we partake in the Determinism attributed to God. Our very being influences what happens in the flow of change that is Existence, so it as well that we try to direct such influence by rational awareness and well thought out intentions. Which brings us on to Providence.

Stoicism also presents God as being Providential and providence is from the Latin 'providere' meaning to 'foresee' or 'to apply forethought' as to what is likely to be the outcome of any choice/physical action. And of course, according to the Stoic rationale the whole of Existence evolves as a result of the 'active principle' (God) determining the flow of change in accord with the laws of nature through choice/rational actions in the Experiential Moment – be it individuals or the Cosmos as a whole that is doing the determining.

Which brings us to one of the aims of the Stoic whereby we are guided to ensure that as many of our choices in life as are possible are thought out (providential) and are not left to the vagaries of the unexamined mind. We are guided to partake in the Providence that is associated with God, by ensuring that we also apply what control/influence we have with forethought - forethought that is guided by our Stoic training to 'live in accord with Nature'. We try, to the best of our individual nature, abilities and circumstance to partake in providently determining the flow of life for the better.

And in the best of Stoic traditions, the emphasis is on physically and mentally 'trying' and not on 'success', in that what turns out to actually be 'success' is not necessarily within our control. That is always the prerogative of 'the bigger picture'.

8. The Stoic's need for a sound mind

'The happy life… is a life that is in harmony with its own nature, and it can be attained in only one way. First of all, we must have a sound mind and one that is in constant possession of its sanity; second, it must be courageous and energetic, and, too, capable of the noblest fortitude, ready for every emergency, careful of the body and of all that concerns it, but without anxiety; lastly, it must be attentive to all the advantages that adorn life – the user, but not the slave, of the gifts of Fortune.'
Seneca On the happy life iii

A sick person does not need a place; he needs medical treatment. If someone has a broken leg or dislocated a joint, he doesn't get on a carriage or a ship; he calls a doctor to set the fracture or relocate the limb. Do you get the point? When the mind has been broken and sprained in so many places, do you think it can be restored by changing places? Your trouble is too grave to be cured by moving around. Travel does not make one a doctor or an orator. One does not learn a skill from one's location. Do you suppose that wisdom, the greatest of all skills, can be assembled on a journey? Believe me, there is no journey that could deposit you beyond desires, beyond outbursts of temper, beyond your fears. If that were so, the human race would have headed there in droves. So long as you carry around the reasons for your troubles, wandering all over the world, those troubles will continue to harass and torment you. Are you puzzled that running away is not helping you? What you are running from is with you. You

need to correct your flaws, unload your burdens, and keep your desires within a healthy limit."
Seneca CIV - On the care of Health and Peace of Mind

There is an ongoing debate as to if we have 'free-will'. The science of the workings of our brains can show that we are already acting before we consciously 'decide' to act as we act. It would appear that matters deep within us have already 'pre-determined' how we are to act in every instance of our lives, albeit sometimes by only a matter of fractions of a second before we become aware that such action has been initiated. Even quite random choices as to a choice between what to drink to quench a feeling of thirst are apparently not spontaneous.

So, as we cannot be fully responsible for what 'pops into our minds', it is necessary to ensure that we are of sound mind and can deal with what 'pops into our minds' as appropriately and as quickly as possible.

But if we are not in total control of what our minds dish up and are not in conscious control of the decisions that our physical brains have already made for us, how can we ever become better than we are?

Without any knowledge of the science of the brain that we have available to us today, Stoicism recognised this problem of 'pre-determined' thoughts and so directed part of the training of the Stoic to concentrate on 'changing their mind'. Stoicism, in its belief that the physics of life is a combination of matter and mind, saw a thought arising in the mind as being an inner action triggered by the physical properties of an 'impression' together with our 'opinions', where the thought is a precursor to further action that will affect the outer world – the world of society.

However, Stoicism teaches us that we have the free-will to 'change' our minds and so change the flow of inner action whereby it does not become inappropriate outer action - provided that we are attentive to what we are thinking and where such is directing us. Our bodies may already be moving towards action in response to this or that by such things as raising the blood flow and by increasing the production of various hormones etcetera. We may even have started to act externally on our thoughts such as blurting out some comment before we have time to consciously think through the consequences, but by the use of conscious reasoned thought we can mitigate, redirect or switch off such sub-conscious induced activity.

At the same time, Stoicism teaches us that, through habituation, we can change the processes that are driving our thoughts. While it is often said that we Stoics believe that we cannot be held responsible for what we think, only for the choices we make in light of such thoughts, in truth Stoicism tells us that we are, once we have achieved adulthood, responsible for the habituation of our deep-down subconscious thought process. Stoicism teaches us to examine our thought processes and to re-habituate our neural pathways by self-indoctrination. And we start to reprogram our minds by settling on a belief system that will form a framework of ideas which will become embedded into the workings of our brain whereby, as much as possible, our thoughts and actions will be governed by such principles – even before we become consciously aware of a situation.

However, Stoicism does not associate the individual's will solely with the workings of the brain. Rather the starting point for all Stoic psychology is that our true consciousness, our will, is the result of our being one with the Whole in that we are manifested by and out of the body of God, where the body of God is the passive Prime Matter imbued with a Single Mind – of which our will is a 'spark'.

And for whatever reason, God has evolved us to have a free will – a will that is part of God's very being and so is inextricably linked to the Whole, but a will that is gifted to us whereby we are free to partake, in accord with our individual nature and our nature as human beings, in the ongoing determination of how matters will evolve in the never-ending flow of change that is Existence. We have been given a free will which makes us individuals in our own right. But regardless of having a free will, Stoicism teaches us that our psychological wellbeing involves us in aligning our free will with the will of God:

'For I regard God's will as better than my will. I shall attach myself to Him as a servant and follower, my choice is one with His, my desire one with His, in a word my will is one with His will.'

Epictetus IV.VII

We are taught to live as we see fit while learning what such means by looking to God for guidance. Such guidance is generally to be found by looking to what God is telling us through the nature of life and all that we find around us.

We look to the Stoic mantra 'Live in accord with Nature' for it is through looking to the design of all around us that we can see the nature of Existence, the nature of the world on which our lives depend, our nature as human social animals, and our nature as individuals with the ability to reason.

We also, in looking to the common perception of all the world faiths, see that trying to live good and honourable lives, so becoming people of good character, is what living wisely involves and that this means aligning our will with the will of the Whole – or in other words, God.

And to this end, so that we may be as consistent as possible in our drive to be the best we can, we keep reminding ourselves of our oneness with God while also looking as to how we can use such knowledge to ensure that our brains are working for us and not against us.

And so we move on to recognising that we have an independent will, a self that can reprogram our minds while also watching over the output of our brains as 'a second line of defence' or to 'offer a second opinion'.

And of course, based on the Stoic view of the physics of existence, our will is more than just the output of our brain. The brain is made out of the same material that manifests the whole Cosmos. But the brain is only part of our being. The whole of our body is made up out of the material that manifests the whole Cosmos, and so our 'spark' of the 'intelligence' that is an aspect of the Cosmos is not limited to the 'matter' that forms our brain. Our will is linked to our whole being, not just to the biological computer contained within our skulls.

As a result, much of the Stoic mind training is aimed at ensuring that we 'act' according to our will, as against acting at the behest of some errant program in our brain that is presenting us with a misperceived impression that has set the brain on pushing for an inappropriate course of action.

For the Stoic, our will is an aspect of who we are, but it is not solely the output of our brains. It is so much more, for it reaches out to the Cosmos and all around us and it can perceive our place within the Whole while seeing that our individual well-being is in truth achieved through putting the well-being of all around us first - whereby we can rest contented that we have 'played our part well' when it comes to the play of life.

Working out what we can reasonably and appropriately do for the well-being of the whole requires that we are able to:

'See things in all their naked reality.'
Marcus Aurelius IV.11

In other words, we need to be able to see reality as it is, and not necessarily as our emotions, instinctive reactions or the programming of our brain may see things. It may be that such inbuilt aspects of our brains do at times see matters correctly, but the Stoic is taught to ensure that such have been properly trained and will answer the rule of reason as applied by our will – our whole self.

Epictetus did a pretty good job of outlining much of the Stoic training methods, but what many forget is that the setting aside of the emotions is only a temporary aspect of the early training of novices. As Epictetus says:

With such high aims, therefore, remember that you must bestir yourself with no slight effort to lay hold of them, but you will have to give up some things entirely, and defer others for the time being.
Epictetus I.IV

From this we see Epictetus telling us that there are some aspects that lead to an unsound mind, such as anger, that are to be avoided for ever and a day. However, there is much that may be deferred 'for the time being' – that is, until such time as the initial stage of our study of Stoicism is over and we are able to start having some degree of rational control over such matters.

Stoicism does not demand that we avoid all emotions or affections for ever and a day, only emotions that are excessive, violent, aggressive, inappropriate and beyond the rule of our will. Calmer natural appropriate emotions, affections and feelings are to be encouraged – just as appropriate love for our children and spouses is encouraged, where the word 'appropriate' is key.

Stoicism recognises that often emotions are triggered by not seeing matters as they are – that is, our impressions can present us with a false image. Many of our instinctive reactions can be triggered by false impressions, such as seeing a shadow cast by a tree as presenting the apparent shadow of a wild animal lying in wait to attack us. And to add to our problems of being able to see reality as it is, the process of the workings of our brains can involve emotionally loaded memories of past events that automatically colour the fresh impressions we are receiving from our senses in the present moment in a negative way, so leading us to react in an inappropriate way.

So Epictetus advises anyone not of sound mind who wishes to become a Stoic to set aside preconceived ideas and avoid any situations that may elicit emotional responses until such time as they have examined the whole of the Stoic teachings and have seen how it all fits together. And such is set aside until the novice has achieved some mastery over their brain. That is, we have to achieve a level of self-control through the use of our reasoning faculty together with a balance between the 'feeling' and 'rational' aspects of our mind – the achievement of which is seen as 'being of sound mind'.

For some the Stoic training will be hard work because of some clinical issue affecting them whereby trying to maintain a sound mind requires more work than most may need. For some, by nature and/or upbringing, what it takes to maintain a sound mind will be the norm and they will experience only minor blips to their normal level state of mind. Whereas for many starting out, they will have need to regain control of their mind from the onslaught of their emotions and their inappropriate habituated mind sets and so will need to work to set the foundations in place while also working through the Stoic mind training.

And for the person who holds back because they think such is beyond them, Seneca reminds us:

'Do you know why we have not the power to attain the Stoic Ideal? It is because we refuse to believe in our power. Nay,

of a surety, there is something else which plays a part: it is because we are in love with our vices; we uphold them and prefer to make excuses for them rather than shake them off... The reason is unwillingness, the excuse, inability.'

Seneca CXVI. On Self Control

9. On Emotional Stability and Attachment

Most problems in everyday life are caused by a person's emotions and their attachments (or even aversions) to people, objects, their own reputation as they see it, and many other aspects of life (the externals).

The Stoic is encouraged to look at their emotions and to see that some are little more than feelings of satisfaction or pleasure that are to be seen as 'affections' or contentment. But the Stoic is also encouraged to be well aware of those emotions and passions that seem to take on a life of their own, those emotions that control one's actions even to the point of blocking out any rational thought. Such emotions can lead the individual into situations that they will later regret. The Stoic will do all they can to avoid letting these emotions taking total control. Self-knowledge, self-indoctrination and training will all help to avoid such emotions running wild. But so also will being constantly aware for the first signs of such. The emotions are there for a purpose – caught early enough and the mind can order them to stand by, and the mind can then rationally assess what started the triggering of the emotions and can then take appropriate action if necessary – but action that is fully under the control of the rational mind.

Where the Stoic does not manage to control the emotion, they will later assess what went wrong and will attempt to set in place a thought (reprogramming) that will come to mind in time to help them avert the problem next time it raises its head. If with practice this does not work, they will learn to avoid, where possible, situations that trigger such an overpowering emotion.

For the Stoic to live the contented life of harmony they see it as being necessary that their rational mind is in control as much as possible, especially regards control of their emotions. While they cannot eliminate the emotions, indeed must not eliminate the emotions, the Stoic will tame their emotions and make them work to their benefit;

never, if possible, allowing such emotions to become uncontrollable passion. A degree of feigned anger may be acted out for the benefit of others as circumstances dictate, but anger must never become the guiding force. Love for others should always be appropriate love so that such love must not divert a person from their duty to their other roles in life.

When it comes to emotions the adage 'all things in moderation' is the real guide – and when it comes to love of a spouse, a child or a friend it will be seen that this can be as deep if not deeper when the emotion is calm rather than when it is out of control.

Many of the causes that trigger emotions are related to what the Stoic calls 'perceptions' and 'attachments' – that is, an emotion can be triggered due to a person believing that they desire a particular person, object or a particular course of action; or an emotion can be triggered due to a fear of perceived loss or suffering. The Stoic overcomes this by recognising that they own nothing and so have nothing to lose. All that they care for is on loan to them from the Cosmos and, by the nature of the Cosmos, all will at some time be redeemed by the Cosmos. Even their own life is on loan to them and, at some point, will be taken from them. This absolute recognition of the transience of all they 'possess' or may wish for is what enables the Stoic to see past their wants, desires, fears and losses, and to look at all around them in a rational manner.

Nothing can take on a greater value to a Stoic than that of the virtuous life living in harmony with all around them. For the only thing that is really theirs is the way they live their life - come what may.

The love of a person should be free of the feeling of possessing. If the loved one is taken away then one must let them go with love. If it is thought that it would be good to have possession of a particular object it must not be reached out for if such will compromise one's duty to one's self and to one's roles in life.

The Stoic, in their mind, separates that which is the paraphernalia related to their various roles in life, from that which is related to their being 'the good actor'. If a particular 'stage prop' is not available to them, the actor will get on without it. If another character takes away a 'stage prop' they have use of, the actor will get on without it. If it appears a particular 'stage prop' might enhance their performance of a particular role they may try to acquire it, always provided that such does not detract from their maintaining the application of their acting skills to that role. If on reaching out for the 'stage prop' the Playwright has decided that they cannot have it, then they will simply accept such and get on with their part in the play. If they are allowed the 'stage prop' they will take good care of it while they have 'use' of it, but be ready to 'lose' it should the Playwright choose to remove it from the stage or pass it to another character.

At all times the Stoic cares for that over which they may have some influence, or which has an influence on their life, while being ready to move on without it. They live without any 'addictive' attachments to anything.

10. The Stoic rationale and 'Emotions' in today's world

The current emphasis on a person 'expressing' their emotions is leading to ever more people with emotional problems in that their emotions are getting out of balance with the rationality of their mind. Much of this is fuelled by talk of the individual's rights and advertising and the like telling people that 'you deserve' this or that. All without the balancing rationality that tells a person that their wants and their needs are two different things. People are not told that they will gain the most by working for the betterment of society and all around them. They are instead being driven into a lonely self-centred existence where their own 'wants' are set above that of everyone else – a state that is liable to lead to increased perturbation. Even spouses and children are now being seen as denying a person their 'rights' and 'freedoms'.

However, Stoicism tells us that we have no 'rights'. Stoicism tells us that we have a 'responsibility' to serve all around us as best we can – and we do this best by ensuring that our emotions are serving us rather than us serving our emotions.

When Stoicism first came on the scene in ancient Greece much of the perturbations people experienced were understandable in that they were reacting to very real threats. In today's world there are still countries and situations where such dangers are as real and in a like manner lead to such things as post-traumatic stress disorder and other disabling mental conditions. And, yes. Stoicism can be a real help in such situations.

But the perturbations that many now feel are to a great deal self-induced, being brought about by following the 'trends' that are encouraging the expression of heightened emotions and excitability together with overly great concern regards self-image while at the same time reducing actual face to face participation with society as a whole.

Where many do show concern for where society is going, all too often such is based on emotional judgements, amounting to perturbations, based on limited consideration of the realities of Nature and the contrary effects that their well-intended actions are liable to have.

There is also the problem of drug abuse in that abuse of drugs is designed to lessen the ability of the reasoning faculty to rule. No Stoic will take drugs with the expressed purpose of 'getting out of their mind', especially as drug addiction is enslavement to an inanimate object. Stoics will only use drugs as is medically appropriate.

The abuse of drugs tends to leave a person with over active free ranging emotions and perturbations that help weaken the individual's ability to apply critical thinking to ideas and situations. An ex-drug abuser who wishes to be a Stoic needs to be extra determined in using all of the Stoic training methods. And when it comes to people who are currently abusing drugs, before they can become Stoics, they need to kick their habit, even if they consider such to be only the so called 'social use of drugs'. The use of cannabis is especially pernicious in that many do not recognise the ongoing damage such does regards one's reasoning faculty's ability to make rational well thought through judgements.

All of which is why Stoicism overcomes perturbations by looking to Nature, wisdom and knowledge in a rationally thought-out manner while ensuring that any natural emotion is answerable to a sound mind governed by a free reasoning faculty. That is, a reasoning faculty that is free in that it is not in thrall of the emotions or external factors, but is able to make judgements as a judge does. That is, with dispassionate consideration of any situation and its context regards self and society as a whole, whereby the 'judge' will not be 'bribed' by any false emotional promise of some questionable benefit that some 'external' may appear to offer.

The 'judge' will make judgements about emotions and choose to allow such to run their course provided the emotions remain answerable to the rule of reason, where such reason has a sound grounding, such as a grounding based in the Stoic beliefs, metaphysics, principles and teachings.

The trained Stoic ensures that their emotions will not be allowed to run totally wild and free of the reigns of the trained reasoning faculty. It is to be ensured that the rational and the emotional aspects of one's thought processes work together in a balanced manner just as a rider and a horse work together as one to complete their journey, where the rider holds the reins and the horse provides the drive.

And in holding the reins, the experienced Stoic ensures that all of their actions, together with their appropriate emotions, will be of benefit to their family, friends and society as a whole and will be appropriate to their roles in life.

Through such is to be found 'eudaimonia'.

Through putting self and one's emotions first is to be found a shallowness of life and perturbation.

The word 'emotion' is used in many Stoic circles today as a direct translation of the Stoic use of the Greek word 'pathos'. This causes many to question the Stoic apparent stance of rejecting all emotions, whereas in fact Stoicism positively encourages what are called 'eupathos' and natural 'affections' etcetera – all of which come under today's catch-all terms 'emotions' or 'feelings'.

Looked at properly it is to be seen that within Stoic writings of old the word 'pathos' with no prefix or suffix is being restricted to talk of 'bad' and/or inappropriate feelings when in fact the Greek 'pathos' simply means 'feelings' – be they good or bad. This use of a single word can cause some confusions, especially if looking at the rationale to be gained from studying the whole of Stoicism.

But as we have a most excellent rule for every phase of life, to avoid exhibitions of passion [pathos], that is, mental excitement that is excessive and uncontrolled by reason
Cicero's De Officiis 136 XXXVIII

Zeno's definition, then, is this: "a perturbation" (which he calls a pathos) "is a commotion of the mind repugnant to reason, and against nature."
Cicero Book 4. On Other Perturbations Of The Mind

Elsewhere, in discussing the Stoic view, Cicero differentiates between 'perturbations' and 'emotions' in general, where 'perturbations' are 'emotions' of a particular quality. As the use of words such as 'passion' (pathos) and 'emotions' have such a crossover in meanings today, so as to avoid ongoing confusion I now follow Cicero's lead and here talk of 'perturbations' and 'emotions' where 'perturbations' will refer to the undesirable feelings that much of the Stoic training seeks to avoid. Perturbations are emotions that are excessive, violent, aggressive and inappropriate and beyond the rule of our will and reason. They tend to be antisocial and lead to actions that are contrary to a life lived in accord with Nature. They can be perturbations of overly heightened and apparently 'pleasurable' excitement or of fear, anger and the like – that is, perturbations relating to excessive feelings of 'attraction' or of 'aversion'. Perturbations are a sign of an unsound mind and so are definitely something that the Stoic wishes to avoid.

Emotions in general are not just internal mental states but are seen as states that are felt as inner movements within the body and are to be seen in the physical stance, body language and facial expressions of the individual. Quite literally an 'emotion' is a visible physical outer expression of the inner 'feelings' that a person is experiencing – which is why Cicero talks of avoiding 'exhibitions of passion'.

Much of the Stoic rationale is based on a 'what you see is what you get' approach. As a result, thoughts are seen to be physical actions or interactions that can be recognised by their physical manifestation, and from such physical appearance is to be ascertained what their character is.

And, generally, our actions manifest as having the character of being rationally led, being led by healthy rational emotions and instincts OR of being driven by irrational perturbations that are out of control.

The Stoics of old looked to the inner 'feelings' as being the internal bodily feeling of being attracted to something, the internal bodily feelings of aversion, together with other such bodily feelings of inner movement that are common reactions to some thought or perception regards something 'external' where such 'feelings' are to be felt in the gut, the chest or elsewhere in the manner of feelings that can still be recognised today.

The Stoic rationale tells us that emotional feelings are not just mental happenings, but they are the body as a whole being affected according to the nature and strength of the feeling.

Many such feelings are simply the result of our natural instincts reacting to receiving impressions of the external world through our senses. In fact, modern sciences show that we have need of such sensitivity to feelings if we are to manage to get on and live life. They provide the drive necessary to get on with life.

By way of the technical language of modern psychology, some talk of emotion/inner feeling as 'affect'. Here 'affect' relates to how an object or situation impacts a person – either through the input of their memory banks or directly in the present moment. Such a sense of 'feeling' is a part of our nature as human animals and is the reaction we feel as our animal self tries to assess our relationship to the ever-changing flow of information that our senses are feeding us. Such feelings are the affect that the outside world has on us through the input of our senses. The feelings that this induces in us are based on processes in the brain and nervous system that make judgements and choices faster than our conscious reasoning faculty can. They are to some extent part of our survival instincts whereby we can react to outside events as quickly as is possible. We are forever playing catch-up with any choices that our body makes before our conscious reasoning faculty has a chance to fully assess the situation.

Naturally, such 'affect' is ongoing and as such the 'feeling' part of our consciousness is using our brain at the same time as is our reasoning faculty. So, as science is telling us, we are constantly living a life that is a balance between the choices that our 'feelings' make and the choices that our 'reasoning faculty' makes.

As it is, much can normally be left to the reactions to our sensory input in that the brain and body are designed to work with such in that we are by nature habituated to react appropriately in accord with our nature as human animals. Basically, we live much of life at the behest of the impressions that impinge our mind together with our instincts and our nature as social human animals.

There are however many things that can fool or pervert our instinctive reaction to life.

There is the classic example of a shadow of a bush being mistaken for the shadow of wild animal lying in wait. Through this it may be seen that our senses do not always serve us well. For instance, it is known that we have a blind spot in our eye and it is only through moving the eye that we can fill in the gap in our vision by overlaying in rapid succession multiple images. If we happen not to be moving our eyes, our brain may fill in the gap in our vision created by the blind spot with what it thinks is probably out there, based on past experience, so it may actually miss something that we need to be aware of and instead lull us into a sense of false security.

In fact, with all of our senses, the brain will fill in gaps in what we perceive, sometimes to amusing effect. Just consider some confusing conversations that can be had with elderly people who are to some extent hard of hearing. Some of the conversations between me and my wife can be hilarious. All of which is why the Stoic is guided to ensure that their 'impressions' are correct by ensuring that they do not go unexamined. We are guided to try to ensure that the information we are receiving through our senses is as good a reflection of the reality of 'what is out there' as is possible.

And that does not just apply to the effectiveness of our senses. When we receive an impression through our senses it travels through the nervous system and the brain and is subjected to various processes whereby it is categorised, assessed against past experience and the like. By the time we are conscious of the impression, not only have the bodily instincts been triggered, but any given impression may have picked up a load of baggage by way of past emotionally loaded experience. Our instinctive drives will also be trying to add to the impression so as to encourage us to follow through in accord with our habituated learnt reactions.

By the time it comes to our conscious awareness, any impression impressed into our mind by the signals from our senses will have become a 'perception' - where we look at 'perception' as meaning 'understanding' in that the 'perception' is an interpretation of the original 'impression' developed by the merging of the impression with our inbuilt and learnt 'habitual opinions' – which often manifest as our appropriate or inappropriate coping mechanism. As such we are constantly being bombarded with the effects of ever fluctuating emotional feelings in that they are for ever reacting to incoming 'impressions'.

When the perception/impression comes to the attention of our reasoning faculty, Stoicism teaches us to unpack all and any inappropriate baggage by way of our training to critically examine such. Despite there being only fractions of a second between our instincts and habituated reactions having triggered our bodily feelings and our getting to grips with any situation through applying our reasoning faculty, more often than not a trained Stoic will be able to put a brake on the development of any inappropriate feelings and so prevent them from getting out of control.

The reasoning faculty is able to re-train errant instincts or inappropriate habituated reactions through rational thought. Science shows that many thought processes in our brains follow well-worn paths – neural pathways. It is known that, through reasoned thought and new habituation, we can lessen the use of some pathways in favour of more appropriate pathways.

In the Stoic training this is done by constantly reinforcing the Stoic framework of beliefs through contemplation and study whereby the beliefs gradually become the thought process that guide all the others. It is also done by trying to maintain as constant a conscious watch on our interaction with all around us as we are able to maintain, both on an ongoing basis and by way of regular self-assessments as to how well we have managed to comply with our chosen standards.

This ongoing reasoned self-assessment of how we ought to have acted, as against how we did act, helps to set road blocks on the undesirable neural pathways. Our instincts and habitualised reactions will evolve over time according to what our reasoning faculty has assessed to be appropriate. We can educate our instincts to lower the threshold at which they will trigger.

As an example, an 'angry person' is a person who has allowed (usually subconsciously) the threshold that triggers their anger to be lower and lower whereby eventually the slightest thing can trigger anger in them. But such can be reversed by applying some discipline and willpower to counter the tendency to get angry over small matters, slowly moving on to greater matters till the tendency to anger is all but eliminated. When the instincts spot any issue coming to their attention that may have in the past elicited the perturbation that is anger, they will instead have learnt to prepare the body for action while holding off from any external action till such time as guidance has been sought from the reasoning faculty as to what is the best way to deal with the situations – whereby any reactive action is carried out because such is appropriate and not because one has become angry.

If past judgements as to what is appropriate have been faulty then we will find that we have errant areas of our instincts and habitualised reactions that work against our chosen moral path. Unless we set about correcting our errant mind-sets, we will have inappropriate feelings and emotions that will affect how we interact with the world about us.

In that errant or appropriate mind-sets are set into place by conscious or subconscious judgements as to what we experience of the outside world, it may be said that what is affecting our mind sets is 'opinion'. And 'opinion' comes down to the issue of wise or unwise use of knowledge or impressions. It is to be remembered that most opinions are learnt - through upbringing or through one's own input. But it is also true that we can change our opinions for the better where necessary, especially as we gain more knowledge and wisdom. And, of course, it is Stoicism's assertion that a good understanding of the Stoic view of our place in the scheme of things and how things manifest as they do is part of what will confirm sound opinions and help to eliminate unsound opinions.

Many emotions express themselves naturally and in accord with the individual's design without any immediate involvement of the reasoning faculty. While the Stoics of old did to some degree recognised such matters, they did not have the science of today that differentiates between what is simply the input of our nature as social human animals and what is the input of our reasoning faculty when it comes to our choices and judgements. That is, there was no real recognition of what goes on in us subconsciously and all talk was of what we are consciously aware of. But in that we also now know that the conscious mind can train the subconscious mind, much of the Stoic ideas regards dealing with emotions still hold.

Generally, emotions and feelings will be instinctual and will be under the control of the choices and judgements of the individual's natural emotion processes. However, when it comes to 'healing' an emotion that tends towards perturbations due to inappropriate historical opinions it is necessary for the Stoic to look to their reasoned judgements and choices and, in the moment, correct any inappropriate habituation of ideas and to ensure that they make fresh judgements and choices based on their examined impressions and examined perceptions - which is where much of the Stoic training for achieving a sound mind comes in.

Even if such is not explicitly part of the Stoic training as passed down to us from yesteryear, there is the saying 'Fake it to make it'. By consciously acting out the natural appearance of a healthy emotion we can cause an unhealthy emotion to fall into line. For instance, it is known that we naturally smile when we are feeling contented and also that we can bring on the feeling of being contented just by smiling.

11. The rationale of the Stoic training

Many tell us that it is a Stoic claim that 'Arete is necessary and sufficient for eudaimonia.' Some reword this to say 'Virtue is necessary and sufficient for eudaimonia.' In both cases 'arete' and 'virtue' are seen as being equivalent to some perfected state that only the impossible sage can achieve. Whereas the Stoic rationale tells us that to a great extent 'arete' and 'eudaimonia' have little to do with what the Stoic is really aiming for.

Stoicism was born into a time when most of the Athenian schools were investigating as to how to achieve and benefit from a state of eudaimonia (good spirits). However, it becomes clear that Stoicism sets a different agenda. Instead, the Stoic's primary aim is to become a good person – a person of good character - through aligning their will with the will of God as best they can. Consequently, the Stoic rationale recognises that 'being of good spirits' (eudaimonia) is just a side effect of achieving some level of success in the true purpose of the Stoic life.

Doing what is right and proper is more important than some self-satisfying 'feeling' a person may personally gain from such action - and in Stoicism doing what is right and proper is to seek to live 'harmoniously' in accord with all else around us, taking into account the 'bigger picture'. This means living in a manner that does not necessarily involve going for the 'obvious' immediate solution, but going for actions that aim for what one may reasonably believe is the path that will prove of most benefit to the whole - such chosen actions being based on wise forethought that is aiming to achieve what is truly of benefit.

In this respect it also has to be remembered that inaction is action in that action or inaction both help to determine how the flow of change pans out. All of which is why gaining an understanding of the degree of influence (control) one can bring to bear in any given circumstance, together with rationally thinking through the likely outcomes of the consequences of such, is an important aspect of the Stoic training.

Our training covers two areas of consideration. As indicated above, the prime one is regards how to physically live life as a 'good' beneficially contributing citizen of the Cosmos and the other is that of acquiring and maintaining a sound mind whereby we can make sound judgements and choices that will manifest as the actions of a person of good character. Of course, the second is a prime requisite if one is to succeed at the former, where success will be that of living in accord with Nature.

So what is a sound mind?

Ideally it is a mind that is in total control of itself and that is not enslaved to anything – but Stoicism recognises that the 'ideal' is not a reality of life. After all, the Stoic rationale teaches us to see things as they are – not as we may wish them to be.

In one respect, some minds are not free of their physical state in that 'physical' disorders (big and small) affecting the mind can lead to all sorts of problems regards self-control. But in that we are not looking to perfection, it is accepted that some people will not have the capability to have as much self-control as others. All, as Stoics, will try to maintain as good a control over their mind and their actions as is possible given their circumstance, while striving, through ongoing training and exercises, to achieve their 'personal best' in their chosen discipline – and that discipline is that of being a good and skilful actor in the play of life.

Much of being of sound mind involves coming to terms with matters that are external to our 'reasoning faculty'. So we need to establish what the 'reasoning faculty' is when it comes to the Stoic monistic view that mind and body are one.

While according to the Stoic rationale our individual consciousness is a oneness that is an aspect of our physical being, it is also to be seen that we can categorise various aspects of the output of our mind while recognising that all aspects operate through their common use of our brain and our nervous system. However, unlike with bodily organs etcetera, there is no definitive boundary between different aspects of the workings of our minds.

There are physical aspects of our brains that appear to be involved in certain physical aspects of our body and thinking processes, however when it comes to the making of choices as a result of the 'feeling' aspects of the mind and the 'reasoning' aspects of the mind there is no real distinction in that in both cases it is our whole self that is making judgements and choices that manifest as action.

As such, this 'reasoning faculty' is in reality a Stoic visualisation that is used as a means to concentrate our minds whereby we ensure that the reasoning and feeling aspects of our consciousness are in harmony and that our emotions do not run away with us. We could just as easily call it our 'Jiminy Cricket' or our 'moral conscience'.

We visualise what it would be like to view 'from afar' how we act within the play of life and what such a dispassionate 'observer' would make of seeing any situation as it really is and what such an 'observer' would judge to be the best way for us to live life. Of course, such an 'observer' ought not to 'feel' our emotions so they are not 'bribed' by such, albeit they may observe them. And so, much of the Stoic training is aimed at distancing the 'reasoning faculty' from the effects of the emotions, and more especially at using its 'distancing skills' to try to prevent any 'feeling' from developing into a perturbation. Despite the rationale of the Stoic beliefs telling us that our nature is monistic, we create an imagined duality of mind in order to ensure that the mind works as a harmonious whole.

While the ability to reason is seen in Stoicism as being what is added to the hierarchy of being – namely 'material' as in all physical 'things', 'animate' as in all living states, 'independently mobile' as in all animal life, 'reasoning' as in all rational beings – living in accord with Nature requires that we acknowledge that our nature extends across all four qualities of being. So when we look to live in accord with our own nature as human animals, as well as to live in accord with Nature as a whole, we are recognising ourselves as human beings that are made out of the matter that is the body of the Cosmos - beings that have the quality of animate life and beings with an element of freedom of movement as well as the ability to reason.

As such the Stoic training is not aimed at just training our reasoning faculty, but at training us to live as physical living independently mobile rational animals that are manifested out of the body of God. We train both body and mind in that they are one.

Which is why learning to keep emotions answerable to the 'ruling faculty' involves both clearing our minds of unsound opinions through rational examination of such opinions, and also habituating our bodies through being aware as to how our body 'exhibits' our emotions through our body language.

For instance, in situations where we are faced with a person who is showing all the signs of being physically threatening, we can add to the problem in that our bodies are liable to mirror their aggression by showing the tenseness of readying itself for flight or fight and such 'exhibition of our emotions' can add to an already tense situation and so bring on an attack that may have been otherwise avoided.

By consciously relaxing one's facial muscles, shoulders and arms and by ensuring that one is not clenching one's fists and the arms are hanging loosely by one's side and that one talks in a calm voice, one presents a non-threatening stance that also says that you are not intending to attack. Concentration on what the body is manifesting helps one to keep calm whereby one is able to ensure that one is thinking rationally and so will be truly ready to act as necessary. Such conscious relaxation of the body language does not reduce one's readiness for action if reason says such is needed. However, often the lack of a threatening response will take the wind out of the other person's sails and they too will unconsciously start to mirror your stance and so will become calmer in themselves.

Some believe that, at times, deliberate aggressive body language may be appropriate – even Seneca hints at such in his views on feigning anger – but here care is needed as the deliberate use of threatening body language will probably heighten one's own inner emotions to whereby the reasoning faculty loses control while stirring up emotions in anyone coming into range of such aggression. This aspect of our nature, whereby emotions are made manifest through body language and body language can affect emotional states, is something that the Stoic needs to be well aware of.

Instead of aggression, the Stoic adds an air of determination to their air of calm as and when necessary - as is exampled in the following report regards Socrates' use of body language:

"But to see Socrates when our army was defeated and scattered in flight at [Delium], was a spectacle worthy to behold. On that occasion I was among the cavalry, and he was on foot, heavily armed. After the total rout of our troops he and Laches retreated together; I came upon them by chance, and seeing them, bade them be of good cheer, for that I would not leave them. As I was on horseback, and therefore less occupied by a regard of my own situation, I could better observe that at Potidaea the beautiful spectacle exhibited by Socrates on this emergency. How superior he was to Laches

in presence of mind and courage! Your representation of him on stage, O Aristophanes, was not wholly unlike his real self on this occasion, for he walked and darted his regard around with a majestic composure, looking tranquilly both on his friends and enemies; so that it was obvious to everyone, even from afar, that whoever should venture to attack him would encounter a desperate resistance. He and his companion thus departed in safety; for those who are scattered in flight are pursued and killed, while men hesitate to touch those who exhibit such countenance as that of Socrates even in defeat.
Alcibiades speaking in Plato's 'The Banquet'

Socrates shows a determined stance, but does not invite attack by 'looking tranquilly both on his friends and enemies.'

All of which is why the Stoic aim of maintaining calm inner feelings while presenting a calm exterior through the rule of the 'reasoning faculty' is sound. And what applies to threatening situations can be of equal benefit in all situations. So part of the Stoic training is to habituate both calm emotions and an outwardly calm physical appearance in all situations whereby the emotions are appropriate and proportionate to the facts of the situation.

In training our 'observer', our reasoning faculty, we learn through the Stoic rationale that its only concern should be to make judgements that will lead to appropriate actions that would be those of a person of good character whose only real interest is to be of benefit to the Whole.

To this end no 'external' has any value to it. The 'reasoning faculty' will not be bribed by some perceived benefit or attachment or aversion. It will judge only as to what is the reality of any given situation. For instance, it will look to the nature of our love for our family members only to consider as to if such love is appropriate and proportionate for a person whose has a role in life to care for their family. From such a stance it will bring its influence to bear by encouraging what is appropriate and/or by trying to reign back on what is inappropriate to a life of good.

And how does it make such dispassionate judgements?

By ensuring that the impressions one is getting from one's senses are as accurate an impression as is possible of the reality of what is happening in our lives. This way, our 'reasoning faculty' will be able to see things as they really are, free from any influence that our emotions may have. As such, by way of example, a spouse or a child is viewed by the reasoning faculty as being a mortal human being that can be physically harmed or taken away from us at any time, while at the same time the individual will still have the natural affections that any healthy human animal will have for their family members.

The view of the visualised 'reasoning faculty' is not in conflict with the view of the 'whole person'. All that happens is that the 'reasoning faculty' offers an alternative view of the same situation whereby we are able to arrive at a sounder understanding of any situation.

So we train to examine the 'naked facts' behind what our senses are telling us and also to examine what our 'opinions' are telling us, especially regards emotionally induced 'opinions'.

In that our true 'reasoning faculty' is the totality of the 'spark of God' that is an aspect of our nature as animals manifested out of the body of the Cosmos, our 'reasoning faculty' is able to rise above many of our excitements, fears or upsets and so continue to help to guide us even in the worst of times. For instance, it can see to it that any natural feeling of loss does not overcome us whereby we cease to be of any benefit to the rest of society.

As Seneca tells us, as Stoics we will feel our hurts but we will overcome or bear them without getting to the stage of suffering perturbations. And we are more likely to overcome or bear them if we keep them in proportion by ensuring that they are appropriate to what it is that is causing the triggering of our feelings. And to do this we look at life from many viewpoints – that of the impressions we receive, that of our instincts and that of our ability to think rationally etcetera. And to help us in all of this we have our framework of beliefs about the nature of Existence that helps to ground our thoughts and actions in the reality of what is.

One of the main Stoic training matters in maintaining a sound mind is that of understanding how to value external things, including people, when it comes to making appropriate choices, especially regards our ongoing choice as Stoics regards being 'good'.

There is a trend to deny that, in Stoicism, anything has any value other than that which maintains the 'goodness' of our 'reasoning faculty'. Yet this is to ignore the Stoic rationale that tells us that God manifests all that there is and that therefore we ought to value all that God has seen fit to present us with through the evolution of the Cosmos. 'What is' is as God wills it to be, so we ought to value 'the gifts of Fortune' - as appropriate.

Restricting value to the 'reasoning faculty' also ignores the Stoic rationale that tells us that our 'reasoning faculty' is one with our physical body whereby we need to maintain the 'goodness' of all 'that is of our doing,' which includes our interaction with 'externals'. And to choose how we interact with 'externals' we need some means of valuing their implications when they impinge on our lives, both regards temptations and regards usefulness.

I need a new car. I am eyeing up a fancy red open top sports car.

Does it have any value regards my being a person of good character. No, but it may make others question my sanity in wanting such a car at my age.

Does it have any value regards fulfilling my needs as governed by my roles in life? Will it help me to fulfil my duties any better than a more sedate sensible and practical car? Probably not. In fact, a more practical car would probably be better in many respects, especially when it suddenly pours with rain.

Is there any reason why I ought to buy the sports car? Maybe I can afford it and I am buying the car as an alternative to my practical car and there is no reason why I should not indulge myself – after all, in buying the car I am providing employment for others and I will be taking advantage of 'the gifts of fortune'.

Is there any reason why I should not buy the car? I cannot afford it and it will affect my ability to fulfil my roles in life, whereby those around me may suffer. And bearing this last point in mind, if I still buy the car it will be because I have placed a 'value' on it that it does not deserve. I will be allowing my emotions to rule my head and this will lead to perturbations, if not immediately, sometime in the future – when, as they say, the chickens will come home to roost. Eventually a solely selfish irrational emotional choice will lead to sorrow.

This is how a Stoic views matters – from many angles, whereby any choice is based on the ratio of importance of many factors.

We are not just looking for how to be 'good', but also as to how to live well in this life we have been gifted.

Above all else, the only thing of real value to the 'ruling faculty' is making choices that will lead to the Stoic being 'good' and to the Stoic being of benefit to society - so aligning their will with the will of God. However, we are not just our 'ruling faculty'. We are rational social animals and as Stoics we aim to live as such. So there is much that is of 'value' when it comes to our being able to fulfil our roles in life. And circumstance will dictate what value we place on such 'externals'.

Traditionally talking of all 'externals' as being 'indifferents' and that such 'indifferents' are 'preferred' or 'dispreferred' can be confusing, especially if you tell a would-be-Stoic that their children are 'indifferents' - albeit that if a child is playing up it might be comforting to think of them as such.

It is better to consider that Stoicism offers two value systems. The first is that which the 'reasoning faculty' needs in order to act as the dispassionate judge, whereby all that it is considering is seen rationally and free of being in the thrall of the emotions. As a judge may look to the justifiability and even the desirability of some 'external', including emotions, when making a judgement, they will be judging as to if and to what extent the involvement of the externals and the emotion is desirable as matters move on. However they will not be swayed by any forceful argument presented by the emotions. The judgement will be about the value of the emotions and externals and will not be a judgement made by the emotions. So the only thing of value to the 'judge' is maintaining a sound mind and having to hand as many examined 'facts' as are possible in order to make sound choices.

Part of making such rational choices will be the ability to judge the relative value of varying factors. And here we have the Stoic value system regards 'externals'.

Now some of the classic examples of looking to the value of 'externals' is health, wealth and reputation. It is clear that all of these are of negative value if such are being used to further the cause of 'bad' people. But for the Stoic, in that we are aiming to be 'good', in almost all circumstance degrees of health, wealth and reputation will be of some value and as such appropriate effort needs to be expended to try to maintain them.

A carpenter will place a value on their tools in that they are necessary for them to fulfil their role as a carpenter. They will place an even greater value on good quality tools that enable them to be at their best. However, if a Stoic carpenter lost all of their tools and could not replace them, they would simply see that their role as a carpenter had been taken away from them – temporarily or permanently.

In like manner, 'externals' have a positive or negative value to us regards whether they help us to serve the greater good or not. But at the same time, even that which obstructs our aims is to be valued as a God given situation, for all is a part of the Cosmos that is manifested in accord with the will of God.

Here we step over into the allied Stoic teachings about acceptance and accepting what is – with gratitude. We also step over into the Stoic teachings about the acceptance of the temporary nature of all 'externals' – even that of our family members in that all humans are mortal.

By seeing and internalising the overarching totally interlinked nature of the Stoic view of life we gradually arrive at the point whereby all falls into place and we are able to mostly live as a 'good' person trying to align their will with the will of God. Occasionally emotions will overpower us. Our training will help keep such incidents to a minimum while also ensuring that we regain control as quickly as possible. For instance, we may feel the loss of a loved one, but our training will tell us that we have not lost the time we did have with them and that we should be grateful for such and that we should move on in our journey just as they have moved on in their journey. And, following the Stoic rationale, if the moving on relates to their death, they will have been reabsorbed into the body of God and so they are still with us.

All such ideas help to lessen any sense of loss and so helps to prevent such becoming a perturbation. And, in like manner, seeing matters from the varying Stoic viewpoints helps us to address all sorts of issues.

As Stoics we can experience all sorts of emotions – however our training ensures, for the most part, that we do not become our emotions.

By protecting our ability to think rationally, by keeping our emotions under control through training, we are better placed to live a life of 'good'. At the same time, by giving voice to our appropriate and proportionate emotions, we ensue that we do not allow our nature as social animals to be perverted into a cold uncaring way of living as is often depicted as being the nature of certain classes of stern and unbending Victorians - those who have given Stoicism a bad name by their unwise rejection of all emotions.

12. Hierocles Concentric Circles and Caring for Mother Earth

Hierocles, a Stoic believed to be from the 2nd century, presented this diagram to suggest that while the animal nature of any animal is to look to their own perceived self-interest, especially in matters that relate to survival, as rational and social animals we also have a need to include in our purview the interests of all the other 'circles' of society that we are a part of.

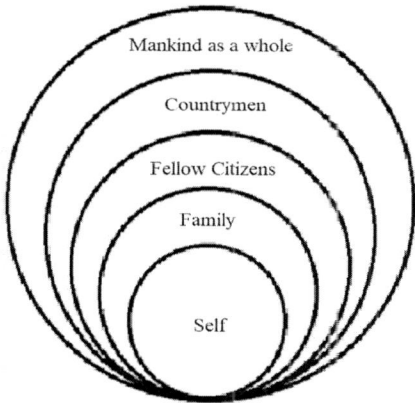

While this diagram in various forms appears in many modern books about Stoicism, as it is presented here it is incomplete unless one sees the space outside of the circle encompassing 'mankind as a whole' as being representative of all else within the Cosmos as well as the Cosmos itself.

The ancients were very interested in the issue of citizenship and our responsibility to not only be of good character, but also to be good citizens who put the interest of society at all of its levels on a par with our individual interests. Effectively Hierocles was guiding the Stoic to mentally draw the outer circles inwards until they all coalesce as the inner circle, whereby we will see no difference between our interests and the interests of any of the other circles.

However, in accord with many of the Stoic ideas, today we need to add another circle that will represent all of the life forms around us and an even larger circle that represents our living planet, Mother Earth, in that we now know that our accumulated individual actions can have an influence on the well-being of our fellow flora and fauna, as well as the well-being of Mother Earth as a whole – while also adding in the largest of all circles to represent the Cosmos as a whole.

And despite such not yet having truly entered into the human psyche, intellectually, we know that if we carry on as we are that eventually the imbalances we are creating will destroy the biosphere that supports us. That is, unless Mother Earth chooses to reduce our numbers through increased 'natural disasters' in order to attempt to rebalance matters whereby she and the life on her surface may have a chance of survival.

Deep down Stoicism has always had a leaning to such ecological matters and as such the Stoic ought to try to reduce their impact by way of including the interests of Mother Earth and her dependents as a whole as being of equal or even of greater importance than their own or human society's selfish self-interest.

From Seneca we have:

'A thatched roof once covered free men; under marble and gold dwells slavery.'

And

'Nature has laid on us no stern and difficult law when she tells us that we can live without the marble-cutter and the engineer, that we can clothe ourselves without traffic in silk fabrics, that we can have everything that is indispensable to our use, provided only that we are content with what the earth has placed upon its surface.'
Seneca XC. On the Part Played by Philosophy in the Progress of Man

And

'God, who is the Father of all, has placed ready to our hands those things which he intended for our own good… But that which would be injurious, he buried deep in the earth. We can complain of nothing but ourselves: for we have brought to light the materials for our destruction, against the will of Nature, who hid them from us.'
Seneca CX. On True and False Riches

Stoicism is predisposed to addressing modern environmental issues. But it is also predisposed to addressing such 'in accord with Nature' – and that means that there is a need to ensure our numbers are controlled, even reduced. I do not remember who, but it is reported that a Stoic of old saw a benefit of war as being that it helped control the size of the population. At the same time the Stoic rationale would discourage wars, especially in that such nearly always elicit the perturbation that is anger. And so the Stoic would have need to come down firmly on the side of population control subject to careful consideration as to how such is to be implemented.

13. Taking the Blindfold off the Judge

Very rarely can a person know all the facts about any given issue, especially as there will be outside influences of which they can have no knowledge. When one's opinions and actions have been based on incomplete knowledge and things do not work out as expected then, unless one should have taken more care and have sought out greater knowledge of the 'available' facts, there is no point in blaming oneself.

One just has to accept what has come to be and then adjust one's knowledge base, one's opinions and one's actions as appropriate and then one gets on with life – a simple principle of acceptance of what is and not wishing for what cannot be, while one continues to strive for the better.

Accepting that what we are presented with within the Now is in fact already part of the Past and cannot be changed is key to a healthy mentality.

Making decisions based on 'what is' and not on one's view of how one thinks it should be is key to a healthy mentality.

Understanding that to fulfil a wish for things to be other than what they are, requires a 'journey' where such a journey requires a clear understanding of the destination; an understanding of the means to complete the journey; an acceptance that there may be diversions on the route and that as time goes on a different destination may become preferable or may even be imposed on one by circumstances beyond one's control; and an understanding that such a 'journey' is not achieved by wishing to arrive at the destination without having 'done' the journey but by taking one step at a time, starting with the first. All this is key to a healthy mentality.

And, of course, striving to be wise in thought and action is key to a healthy mentality.

This all leads into considering the areas over which we can have some influence and degrees of control. Dissatisfaction with life and feelings of helplessness (non-clinical depression) are usually the result of not facing the realities of life.

The main areas that can blind the 'judge' to the realities of life generally come under the headings of: Addictions, Untamed Emotions and Indoctrination.

To counter the problems that addictions, emotions and indoctrination can cause, processes are needed to help us make good judgements and these are seen as: Awareness, Preparedness and Reasoned Belief.

And having removed the blindfolds from the 'judge' and in seeing things for what they are, one is able to move onto achieving: Freedom of Mind, Right Living and Contentment.

So at a glance we have the purpose of dealing with that which blinds one's rational mind (the 'judge') to the realities of life:

Move from	Move to	Achieve
Addiction	**Awareness**	**Freedom of Mind**
Untamed Emotions	**Preparedness**	**Right Living**
Indoctrination	**Reasoned Belief**	**Contentment**

Addictions

By not seeing life as it really is we can cause ourselves much misery and miss opportunities for much enjoyment. It is obvious that in the use of any substance that is mind or mood altering that we are perverting our rational thinking processes – and in such circumstances it is all too easy to become addicted to not seeing life as it really is.

But it is not just the abuse of drugs that can become an addiction and so lead to misery. How many people are addicted to money and will ruin their lives in the pursuit of it by giving it a sense of value other than as just a means to barter for what is really useful in their lives. How many people so value money that they will destroy their marriages and their relationship with their children, will destroy all trust that others may have in them, and will even destroy their own future contentment in its pursuit.

A person can become addicted to almost anything. Here, 'addiction' is the inappropriate wanting to possess or to have control over something – be it money, a car, or even a spouse - to the point where one's addiction becomes one's slave master. One can even be addicted to an idea, gradually moving from having a thought to feeling the need to implement that thought no matter how irrational or harmful such action may be.

While much may not have the chemical hold that drugs can have when they cause addiction, it is the same lack of rational thinking that leads to a person turning to drugs for the first time that leads to a person starting to pursue other things in life in an addictive manner.

The understanding that the Cosmos is manifested by a single 'Consciousness' leads a person to realise that all that they yearn for, all that they strive for, is manifested by the 'Cosmos'. So one may see that all that comes into one's life is not for one to possess, but is on loan from the Cosmos. It is also obvious that "what the Cosmos gives, the Cosmos **will** take away".

Through the process of life and death, creation and renewal, everything in life is transient. Everything that is not-self, including one's body and one's life can be, and eventually will be taken away. If one becomes addicted to anything, not only will such a state of mind divert one from living life well but one will eventually suffer when it is taken away, and will probably have suffered in one's efforts to possess and keep it.

Addiction is inappropriate attachment.

It is appropriate to love one's spouse and so to be attached to them — that is what marriage is. It is a formal process of a couple declaring that they are appropriately 'attached' to each other in accordance with the 'marriage contract'. Love should not be a declaration of possession.

Possessiveness leads to jealousy, abuse and all sorts of other actions that will kill off any love that there is. Through an inappropriate attachment to a partner one will cause pain and will suffer pain. Through the appropriate attachment, whereby one is aware that one's partner is not one's possession but is 'on loan' from the Cosmos, one will live for what the relationship brings to one's life within the Experiential Moment, always knowing that what one has 'on loan' can be taken away at any time.

One can live in hope of a future with one's spouse, but for one's own sake and for the sake of one's partner one must accept that that future may not happen.

With life lived in the Experiential Moment, what one has in the Experiential Moment is all that one has. One has this moment with one's loved one. One has one's memories of one's time with one's loved one in that this is an aspect of the unchangeable past. One does not have a future with one's loved one for the future does not exist, so it is always best to make the most of the present moment while still planning for the future. If one loses one's loved one, provided one has loved them for their sake, and not as an addiction (that is selfishly) one will be able to let them go with love. One will still miss them, but one will not undo the happiness one had – no loved one would want you to suffer over their loss. They would want you to celebrate your time with them while wishing them well on their journey.

And what applies to a loved one, applies to all that comes into our lives.

'Appropriate attachment' is to care for that which one has in one's life while accepting that life is a process of change. Through 'inappropriate attachment' one could spend all of one's life trying to hold onto what one has on loan, only to then lose it all by dying. Living so, one would not have lived a life in enjoyment of what one had – a journey that one can appreciate, a journey shared for some of the way with one's loved ones, a journey free of addiction so that one can make the most of one's life.

At all times, regards all that is in one's life, one should look to ensure that one has not got into an inappropriate attachment:

Does what you have in your life and how you think of it affect adversely your performance of your life roles?

Have you put anything, including your faith, on a pedestal whereby it is diverting you from performing your life roles to the best of your ability?

Is a role that you have taken on diverting you from more important roles such as being a spouse, a parent, a family member, a citizen of the Cosmos?

Are you seeing anything through rose tinted glasses and not seeing its real effect on you and the rest of the Cosmos?

Are you 'selling' your very Self, your honour and judgement, in order to possess something?

Are you ready to let go of anything that you have on loan, including your life, should the Cosmos choose to take it back by whatever means?

(Always remembering that where you have care of something, in matters such as theft, it is acceptable to try to prevent the loss, but if you are unable to, if you had an appropriate attachment to what is lost, you will be able to move on with life without undue regret.)

These are all examples of the sort of questioning that will highlight as to if your attachment to what is in your life is appropriate or inappropriate.

Just as one would not abuse drugs in the first place and so get addicted to them if one had foreseen how they would adversely affect one's life and had realised just what cost they would have regards one's rationality and judgement, by seeing things for what they really are, by seeing the appropriateness they have to the performance of your roles in life, and by accepting that nothing is worth enslaving your Self, so one will be able to have an appropriate relationship to them and be able to let them go when it is necessary or appropriate.

You always have a choice – a life of freedom or a life of self-imposed enslavement

Emotions

Just as a rider will sometimes let the horse roam as it chooses, at other times will gently guide the horse by means of the reins, and at others will take full control of the direction they are moving in, so a person should be to their emotions. The emotions are part of our nature and so have to be accepted. But we also need to try to ensure that the emotions serve us and do not 'bolt' like a spooked horse, leaving us to cling on for dear life.

We should at all times try to ensure that our emotions remain relatively calm, while observing what the triggering of heightened emotions is telling us. We are advised to try to avoid our emotions running wild and so reducing our self-control. The threshold at which an emotion is triggered and the degree to which it will make itself felt can in most cases, if needed, be controlled by practice and training.

Just as a rider takes a wild horse and tames it, so we should take our wild emotions and tame them.

The problem when addressing emotions is that they are not a singular phenomenon. They are the coming together of many aspects of the mind and instincts in various combinations, and in some cases the release by the Body of 'chemicals' into the system.

Not even the experts can agree on the details regards the nature of emotions, so we cannot be expected to fully understand them either. It might help to remember that the original root of the word 'emotion' suggests a meaning of 'the outward signs of an inner stirring'.

Certainly there are some emotions that are perfectly acceptable in almost any circumstance but what we are looking to tame are those emotions that lead to or are caused by addiction, and those emotions caused by our ancient instincts that seem able to swamp our brains and to drive out all rational thought. We are trying to prevent the 'emotions' becoming 'the outward effects of an inner storm'.

If we are lucky our parents and educators will have helped to train us during our youth through teaching us self-discipline, manners and a sense of right and wrong. They will have tried to dull the less desirable aspects of our burgeoning character through appropriate discipline.

They will have tried to enhance the more desirable aspects of our burgeoning character through appropriate encouragement and even reward. They will have tried to tame us, rather than leave us as feral animals. Not to have tried to do so is tantamount to child abuse.

At a point it is necessary for each of us to take over the ongoing taming of our emotions, for not all emotions retain the same power during the whole of one's lifetime. The development into adulthood and the aging process affects the nature of the emotions. Circumstance and any overload on the triggering of our emotions can change the effect that emotions have in our lives. The training and guiding of the emotions is a lifelong process aimed at ensuring that, in an appropriate manner, the rational mind can take the reins and keep the emotions under a reasonable level of control.

There are some very well-tried practices for taming the emotions – all that is required is some willpower. That is, we need to be willing to put in the effort needed to habitualise and see through beneficial decisions.

As soon as one becomes aware that an emotion is stirring, one ought to check it out by use of the rational mind – if it is pleasant and unlikely to cause harm, go with it if such is appropriate. But beware that the 'judge is not bribed'. If an initial cursory check sees something as 'pleasant' it may be because the emotions have already taken control of one's mind or that it has become an addiction. With practice we can develop an aspect of the conscious mind whereby, even when the emotions are taking the lead, the conscious mind has an ongoing role as an 'observer' – an 'observer' that is ready to step in and take back the reins at any time.

The 'observer' is most useful when the emotions are not very desirable ones. As with all emotions, the observer will be looking at the facts of any given situations and not just the view the emotions are suggesting. The emotions are often the results of some initial simple trigger buried in our 'programming' – our built-in animal instincts and our experiences. We may just be seeing some similarity between a current event and a past experience that involved an emotion and this link in the mind may stir up the emotions. We may be seeing an incomplete picture being based only on an initial subconscious 'glance'.

It is the job of the 'observer', the rational mind, to take a second look and to decide whether to go with the emotion's suggested course or if to use the 'cold light of day', that the rational mind can shine on an event, to stand the emotion down. Even when it has been decided to run with the emotion, the 'observer' must be ready to take the reins again if needed – both to temper and guide it or to divert it and dissipate it. Consider the old saying, 'Too much laughter will lead to tears.'

Training oneself as above on the little things will help one to keep control when the stronger emotions, such as anger, rear their heads. Over time if left unchecked, that which will trigger a heightened emotion will need less and less 'power' – in an 'angry person' the failure to attempt to control their anger will mean that they will lose control and in time will let anger take control for the least of reasons.

In extreme situations 'blind emotions' may give one the power to do what one would or could not normally do. The emotions are there for a reason – some of them are there as part of our survival tools. But because we do not live in a natural animal way anymore, we often find our emotions being triggered inappropriately. So we need to have some level of rational control at all times – then, if it is really appropriate, we can temporarily relinquish control and leave the survival instincts to do their job.

However, when we find that a survival instinct has been triggered it is probable that the Body will already have pumped chemicals into the system to enable the Body to act in ways that will ensure the Body's survival (or even, at the risk of death of one's own Body, the survival of one's family or perceived 'tribe'). If the rational mind is able to retain control and prevent the mind being swamped by the emotion, or even if it may have lost but regained control, in order to help the emotion to stand down and in order to keep the Body healthy, the person will need to dissipate the 'chemicals' that have flooded their systems.

Usually the 'chemicals' are aimed at some form of action and so almost any activity will help dissipate or use up the 'chemicals' and so bring the Body back to an even keel. Sometimes, especially in the early stages of an emotion being triggered, the energy used in rational thinking will be sufficient to switch off the supply of energy inducing 'chemicals' and to use up what has been injected into the system. But usually if the emotion is aiming at producing a particular form of activity, such as fight or flight, then as soon as possible it is advisable that one diverts the heightened energy into some more benign and appropriate form of action – such as using a punch bag, going for a long walk or having a cold shower. Each person will in time find what works for them.

Just living in a modern society gives cause for the emotions to be constantly trying to trigger some form of action – this is why physical activity is so desirable. Something as simple as regular walks can be sufficient to work any build-up of the triggering chemicals out of the system. Certainly, some triggering of the survival instincts is desirable so as to keep the body in good shape – hence sports and other forms of risk taking. However, one has to be careful not to take matters too far – if one is to retain a level of rational control one does not want to become addicted to adrenalin and the like

As with everything, when it comes to the emotions it is all a matter of 'all things in moderation'.

With a horse, in order to get a good ride and to be able to bring it back under control if it gets spooked, one needs to ensure that it has been properly tamed and that it will trust your decisions as the rider and so will obey your commands.

So it is that the emotions need to be tamed and need to be able to trust the decisions of the rational mind. The more the rational mind successfully exercises control, the more the emotions will work with it and do their jobs correctly. The more the rational mind ensures the less desirable emotions are not triggered unnecessarily the greater will be the trigger needed to set them off – so leading to a more pleasant contented life.

And where a person finds a particular type of situation always triggers an emotion, such as anger, it will probably be because at some time in the past a traumatic situation has 'tied' the emotion to that type of activity. Such will need careful handling to try to untie the link of emotion to event or even, in extreme cases, there will be the need to avoid any activity that is known to trigger the emotion no matter how much one tries to rationally act otherwise.

We cannot suppress all emotions – we can only tame, educate and guide them so that they serve us rather than control us.

Indoctrination

Much regards our beliefs, our traditions, and our very character is the result of indoctrination. This is not necessarily a bad thing. It helps us to fit in with the rest of society, and also to be able to have a framework of ideas that will guide us in living our lives without having to think out every aspect of our actions and interactions.

A core influence on our nature as individuals is based on the human species' animal nature, but within each individual, in some aspects, this animal nature will be more or less emphasised, or may even be 'damaged' due to fluctuations and faults in the genes. All part of what makes us 'individual'.

Another influence is the early experiences while still in one's mother's womb and the first couple of years as a child. During this time the brain is developing at an extraordinary rate, and all that is experienced is effectively hard wired into the thought processes because such experiences are affecting the development of the brain by emphasising certain connections within the brain.

From then on, throughout childhood, our own experiences, influenced by our developing character, will reinforce or weaken various aspects of our nature according to what we believe to be apparently our best course through life. The influence of others, especially respected family members or friends, as well as events, will affect our opinion of life and how to live it. We will be subjected to cultural and, usually, religious influences. The nature of our games will have an influence – it is said that a child's play is their work. It is part of their learning process, and the nature of the play can have a profound influence on our view of life.

Basically, life and everything in life is a process of indoctrination, in so far as indoctrination is us being influenced by experience or people in a way whereby we are not necessarily in control of the effects it is having on us. This is why child abuse is such a horrendous crime, bearing in mind child neglect and neglect as to the influences that a child is being subjected to can be as much child abuse as is physical abuse.

Into the teenage years, and a person has to cope with the changes in their body and the resultant rampaging hormones. For some this will be a fairly gentle process, for others it will almost tear them apart. Their early years will have an effect as to how a person copes with their puberty and continued brain development, the brain usually only stopping physical growth at about the age of eighteen to twenty-one.

So by the age of twenty-one a person's character, as a result of 'nature and nurture', will have, for the most part, become fairly set within the 'hardwiring' of the brain. However further 'indoctrination' can take a hold even after this.

Clearly it is desirable that, as a child, one's parents should have guided one to such influences that would develop one's character, strengthening the good points, while 'dulling' the less desirable points, especially the aspects of character that came with the genes. (Without such influence a child is liable to remain a 'feral animal', which will detrimentally affect their adulthood.) Positive 'indoctrination' (including both appropriate praise and appropriate punishment) is a desirable aspect of one's early learning years, it generally being recognised that most good, or even harm, can be done in the first seven years, and that what is learnt in the first thirteen years will help one through the years to maturity. But from thirteen, if one's hormones will allow it, and certainly from the age of twenty-one, it is for the individual to control the nature of any 'indoctrination' they may be subjected to.

So we are encouraged to look at our character and our nature and to understand how it has developed to the stage we are at. There is much of one's character that one has to accept, for as was said, much will be effectively hardwired into one's brain. However, there is also much that is down to the indoctrination of one's early years, and this can be 'corrected' if needed by counter-indoctrination – self-indoctrination through understanding and training or retraining.

We need to become our own indoctrinator. We will examine our character, and will try to moderate its extremes by training ourselves to stop and think when it comes to areas where our character might normally lead us into paths that are against our chosen path. We will look at the habits of thought and action that our past 'indoctrination' has set in place and, where necessary, will set about changing or adapting the habits in order to be in better control of our lives.

Where a person's parents have not trained them properly in childhood due to neglect or just a lack of understanding, or where circumstances have had adverse effects, as an adult, as and when they become aware of the negative effects on aspects of their characters or indoctrination, the person is encouraged to stop and take time to retrain themselves in such aspects.

To try to control what outside influences we take on board we will try to avoid situations where individuals or groups are trying to indoctrinate an audience or such like, or at the least we will ensure that we do not get caught up in any group excitement by retaining a critical observance of all that is being said and the manner in which it is being presented – we will ensure that our 'observer', our conscience, our 'Jiminy Cricket' is sat securely on our shoulder. Only after due consideration ought we to take on board or reject the influence of others.

If we spend all of our lives examining moment by moment what we are thinking and doing we will not be able to get on with life. We need to live much of life on 'autopilot' – we therefore need to be sure that the 'autopilot' is properly programmed and that there is a 'pilot' ready to take back control as and when necessary. Our 'observer' needs to be on hand at all times.

We are also encouraged to spend time honestly reviewing our lives since the last review to see where we may not have come up to the standards of thought and action we have set ourselves, so that we may practice in our mind how we could have acted better so as to train ourselves to do better next time, where appropriate. And where we have got things right, we can pat ourselves on our back so as to encourage future proper thought and action. Such a review ought to be carried out at least once a day, preferably last thing at night while matters are still fresh in the mind.

Awareness

Addictions, emotions and indoctrination can all lead to life problems – the solution is awareness. Awareness is ensuring that one's 'observer' is awake and on the job.

Lack of awareness is typified by the child/mother game whereby the child asks the inattentive mother a number of questions that would all elicit the answer 'yes' if the mother were being attentive. Having started to get affirmative answers the child then asks what they are really interested in – can they go out to play, can they have a sweet, can they stay overnight at a friend's place. They believe that their mother would normally say 'no' if she were being attentive. But they are using her lack of full attentiveness and, by creating a norm reaction to the earlier questions, they hope to get the answer they want – yet another 'yes'.

Try to be aware of what is going on around you and within you. One is never going to be one hundred percent aware all of the time, but one can be sufficiently aware not to run through life continually on autopilot. Our attention is more geared to noticing things that change suddenly than it is to that which has become a constant within our lives. Because of this we can start to 'take things for granted'. We may not see a situation where it has crept up on us slowly. One may not notice 'the wolf in sheep's clothing' if one has become used to seeing sheep all around.

Awareness is to examine what is really going on, as against what one believes may be going on. Look under the clothing to see if one has a sheep or a wolf.

What appears to have been a good idea on a number of occasions may not be the next time. We need to live as much as we can in a state of awareness. In particular we need to be aware as to where our thoughts are leading us or may have led us into inappropriate situations. And where our lack of awareness has led us into turning a thought into an inappropriate action, we need to review what has happened in our lives – all part of our ongoing training.

As said, one cannot be aware at all times, but with practice one can learn to be aware as much as possible so as to avoid slipping into addictive ways, to have as much control over the emotions as possible and so ensure that one is not allowing others to have undue influence over one's thoughts and actions.

Just as the tightrope walker should have a net ready to catch them, so spontaneity needs a cool, calm and wise 'observer' ready to take control if needed.

The person going bungee jumping may believe that they are being adventurous, but they would be foolish to try it if they did not know that the equipment had been well designed and safety checked, the site had been well chosen and that there is someone there to ensure everything goes as it should.

Spontaneity really does need a lot of planning.

Preparedness

People are advised to use their imagination and to prepare themselves so that they are ready to cope with future events.

A classic Stoic example is that of going before a powerful man – we are advised to practice in advance in our mind how the 'interview' may proceed. Consider the man - see that he is only a man; see that the man and his position are two different things; consider the respect the man has earned and the respect that his position should be given; consider his power - against proper training and forethought this is nothing. Practice imagining being at ease in his presence; consider possible scenarios as to the progress of the meeting. By such preparedness one is liable to be better able to maintain one's composure, and so will therefore be most liable to get the most from the meeting.

And this applies to many aspects of life. One should be prepared not just for the normal events of life, but for any sudden changes in fortune. To suddenly come into a lot of money a person will be pleased, but they should not let such affect their inner contentment. To suddenly lose all that one has - one should be equally unaffected for one will know that due to the vagaries of life such can happen at any time. One may be sad at the loss of loved ones, but such will be kept within bounds and one will quickly return to one's inner state of contentment, for one will have practiced the possibility within one's mind in advance and will be ready to accept such - and so the event will be no more than a brief shock.

Faced with a flood or an earthquake, a person will use all of their self-training to try to remain calm and to look for any opportunity to serve the greater good – if possible, attempting to save the lives of those around them, even at the risk of their own life. This does not mean that every person will be courageous – rather that they will overcome their fears, and make the best possible judgements regards the situation.

Obviously untimely death is often considered to be a calamity, especially to the one dying. So a person is advised to prepare themselves as best as possible to accept their own death no matter when it comes. But they will not throw their life away needlessly. Circumstances will mostly dictate. For example, to stay behind and die that others may live or to calmly take the lead and to lead others to safety – the prepared person will know their strengths and weaknesses and will decide accordingly.

While it is not possible to prepare for every event, using the imagination to see oneself being calm and collected in the worst of possible situations will help one when faced with real situations to actually remain calm and collected.

To this end the most important aspect of being prepared is summed up in two words – a classic quote – 'Know Thyself'. A person is well advised to look honestly at themselves and to know their own strengths and weaknesses. A person is advised to try to be the 'craftsman' when it comes to life, and as such they need to know how to use the tools they have to hand. The individual person's tool is their own self.

All of the self-indoctrination, study and learning, attentiveness and preparing is the honing and care of the tool they have to work with. The actor will spend a lifetime developing their skills in order to become and remain an actor that will enhance any play.

Reasoned Belief

What is 'real'? What are 'facts'? What is 'knowledge'?

Unfortunately there is no definitive answer as to what is real, what facts are and what knowledge is. All that we can 'know' is at best an approximation. Even scientific knowledge is simply the best rational ideas for what it is that the scientist is observing – or at least it ought to be. But what is deemed to be scientific fact today will be improved on or rejected as the skill of the scientists moves scientific belief forward to, hopefully, better understandings.

Everything that we think we know is just opinion and belief.

There is a fun philosophical challenge. Consider the suggestion that the whole Universe was created and 'switched on' just two hours ago. The normal challenge to such an idea is 'But I can remember what happened three hours ago, a day ago and so on, so it must have been around for more than two hours.' To which comes the answer, 'All of your memories that appear to suggest a life before the Universe was switched on are false memories – they had been built into you as part of the Creation that occurred just two hours ago.'

In this mental game, it does not matter if the Universe was created two hours ago or if it has always been. Even if our memories and acquired understanding of life never actually happened, it is reasonable to assume that these were built in for a purpose so it would be rational, indeed advisable, to pay heed to what we believe and to treat such as true.

For instance, in assuming that the Cosmos was not created two hours ago, but is eternal, it is reasonable to pay heed to what we believe we know and to treat such as true until such time as we discover otherwise.

When it comes to science, many ideas hold sway for years, even decades, before being challenged or improved. When it comes to the Religions, while these appear to have been around for hundreds of years, they also have been challenged or 'improved' – often leading to them splitting into sects. In some cases religious sects have been so called 'improved' to the point whereby they have ceased to follow the faith that was the foundation to their existence. The evolution of the Conway Hall Ethical Society is just such an example where it moved from being a protestant religious group to being an organisation promoting secular humanism. We even have groups who claim to be Christian Atheists.

So when it comes to what it is reasonable and rational to believe, the Wisdom of the Ages is trusted as a guide. Such wisdom is that which is the wise belief to be found across all ages, cultures and faiths and which are those beliefs that have stood the test of time worldwide over thousands of years.

It is through looking behind the differences in wording and visualisation and seeing the common ground that the manifestation and the nature of the Cosmos is to be discovered.

This thinking is both reasonable and rational, in part being based on a statistical approach, but also because it is based on experience.

Freedom of Mind, Right Living and Contentment

Freedom of mind and right living are all down to thinking for oneself and living according to one's knowledge and beliefs in light of the awareness of the metaphysics that states that we are all part of one living conscious Cosmos – that is, that we are manifested out of the body of God.

Many see the solution to many problems as seeking 'happiness'. But if they are not careful, they can be led astray and find themselves looking for something that cannot be controlled. The root from which the word 'happiness' comes is 'hap' - a root word associated with luck. 'Haphazard' - left to chance, with no control. 'Hapless' - unlucky. 'Happening' - an event that has little or no planning. 'Happenstance' - something that happens by chance, coincidence.

So the word 'happiness' clearly is associated with luck, and so is not something that can be planned for despite many a book trying to offer a plan that will supposedly lead to 'happiness'. There is the popular guide to finding happiness - 'Happiness is like a butterfly. The more you chase it, the more it will fly away and evade you. But just sit down quietly on a rock, and it will come and settle on your shoulder.'

Happiness in this context is usually the coming together of events whereby a feeling of pleasure and completeness sweeps over one. However, for most people, happiness is the elation that is triggered by the release of hormones within the body as the result of some event or action where the body feels it needs to alter its mind set in order to cope with the situation. But such elation is usually followed by a negative state of the emotions - leading to the ups and downs of the emotions that it is preferable to avoid.

One can go on and on with example after example, and all would prove that 'happiness' is not a very good feeling to <u>aim</u> for. The present-day idea of 'contentment' is a more appropriate feeling to try to develop, its root being associated with completeness, that which is contained, and that which makes up the whole. 'Contentment' is associated with calmer emotions than 'Happiness'.

So what would characterise the person who achieved a more or less constant state of contentment? The contented person will have stable emotions, they will be at one with the whole of existence, and they will accept their situation within the whole, while striving to ensure that they play out their roles in the play of life to the best of their ability. Contentment is being at one with the whole and being at one with oneself.

And all of this is within a person's control. Emotions can be trained to be calm. An understanding of the whole and one's place within it can be learnt. An understanding of what life is liable to bring one's way, and what of this is within one's control, can also be learnt - so helping one to know what one should accept as it is, and what one should accept and then work towards changing - if it is one's role to bring about such change. And the choice to fulfil one's roles to the best of one's ability is certainly within a person's control, provided they have a sound awareness of the nature of life, and a sound life philosophy. This is the Stoic science of the psychology of a contented life.

14. Aretê, Character and the Good

When it comes to the study of Stoicism, discussions often swing back and fore between the use of modern English, Latin and ancient Greek and in the process the original intent of the Athenian Stoics can be overlooked.

An important term within Stoicism is the Greek word aretê which refers to 'excellence and goodness of character' (later aligned with the Latin word 'virtue').

Of course, the word 'character' is derived from a Greek word that carries the same meaning that our modern equivalent does today. 'Charaktíras' refers to the nature of something.

When it comes to what we moderns see as 'goodness', the ancient Greeks in fact referred to as 'the good' within the make-up of something, in that they saw this as referring to physical characteristics that were to be known through observation. It is to be remembered that Stoicism is based on a strict materialistic view (albeit the specific Stoic view of materialism).

So key to much of the Stoic teachings is that the would-be-Stoic has decided that they want to physically manifest 'excellence and goodness of character' and they do this by emulating what is seen as the 'common perception' of how a person of good character would be recognised through their outer physical actions.

There is a Stoic expression, popular amongst modern would-be-Stoics that 'aretê is necessary and sufficient for eudaimonia'. In today's speak we would say that a person of excellent good character will live in such a manner that they will be justifiably contented with how their lives impinge on all around them and how all around them impinges into their life. Through such contentment comes a feeling that everything is right in the world – which is the real intent of the word 'eudaimonia' for the Stoic.

The Greek word 'eudaimonia' translates quite literally as 'good spirits' which, as Zeno defined it, is the feeling that one is living 'in the smooth flow of life'. If translated as 'happiness', as many translate 'eudaimonia' today, then there can be misunderstandings and the aim of being a person of excellent and good character can be lost from sight.

But to return to 'aretê' as 'excellence and goodness of character', when looking at a knife the Athenians saw 'the good' as the characteristic of that knife that includes such matters as its design being fit for its particular purpose, the comfort with which it sits in the user's hand, how it benefits the skill of its user, it being in good condition as well as being well honed and presenting a pleasing appearance, etcetera. As A A Long explains in his book 'Stoic Studies', we are looking at 'the good' in an item as being an observable set of harmonious characters, and such is seen as 'excellent' (aretê) when all the appropriate characters are present and exist in harmony with each other – the Greek expression being that 'all the numbers are present'.

So the Stoic trains to develop 'the good characters' in order to be able to be 'excellent' (skilled) in the living of their lives for the purpose for which they are put on this earth – just as a knife is excellent when it serves its purpose on many levels. However, the knife is not 'excellent' for its own sake. It is only 'excellent' when it is serving its purpose for being.

And here Marcus Aurelius tells us:

VIII.59. 'Mankind have been created for the sake of one another.

V.1. 'Consider each tiny plant. Each little bird, the ant, the spider, the bee, how they go about their own work and do each his part for the building of an orderly Universe.'

III.13. 'Thou shalt never carry out well any human duty unless thou correlate it to the divine.'

We are not told that the Stoic's efforts at manifesting the 'good characters' is for our own self-satisfaction or for us to achieve 'eudaimonia'. The self-improvements are always aimed at being of service to our society, our world and to God. The feeling of 'eudaimonia' is just a side-product. 'Eudaimonia' is never the end target for the Stoic.

The living as a person of good character whereby we aim for our will to be one with the will of God is the target. And if a person does not believe in this target, but is more interested in their selfish wants, they will not advance as a Stoic.

15. Thinking like a Stoic

If one believes in the Stoic metaphysics and its rationale then many issues will be seen from a different perspective to that which is prevalent today.

All too often ideas are centred around some simple slogan that is meant to encapsulate some way of seeing life in a manner that will supposedly be of benefit to 'the individual' should such ideas come to fruition. However, such tends to lead people into 'camps' that start demanding that the whole of society should adapt to follow their minority view – a view that is often not based on a rational overview of the nature of life as a whole and that often leads to a 'them and us' outlook that is contrary to the 'inclusion' that such ideas are meant to engender in the whole of society.

Naturally we Stoics do not think that we are going to fall into such a way of thinking despite the fact that we are united in the acceptance of the simple slogan, 'Live in accord with Nature' where we see Nature as the manifestation of the will of God.

What hopefully prevents us from believing that everyone else <u>must</u> convert to <u>our</u> way of thinking is our belief that each person must think matters through for themselves - rationally according to their nature - and not to follow blindly. As to if a person is unable to accept the Stoic view of the God that is revealed through the Stoic metaphysics, and instead has other beliefs, this is not the concern of any individual Stoic. The Stoic's only concern is that they themselves live up to their chosen beliefs.

Stoicism is not a belief system that is enhanced by seeking to convert others to Stoicism. 'Quality rather than quantity' is the watch word. As Mahatma Gandhi is reported as saying,

"I came to the conclusion long ago that all religions were true and that also that all had some error in them, and while I hold by my own religion, I should hold other religions as dear as Hinduism. So we can only pray, if we were Hindus, not that a Christian should become a Hindu; but our innermost prayer should be that a Hindu should become a better Hindu, a Muslim a better Muslim and a Christian a better Christian."

The Stoic's aim is to become a better Stoic. It is not to convert others to Stoicism.

OK, we write about our faith and 'put it out there' for others to consider. Primarily we write for ourselves in order to clarify our own individual take on Stoicism and hence how we are choosing to try to live our lives. At the same time, we are trying to keep Stoicism alive in that we do not see it as some professors see it – as an 'interesting' ancient philosophy that supposedly died out when Christianity came on the scene. For the Stoic, Stoicism is still very much alive and relevant to life today.

Through offering our views and through reading the views of other Stoics we share our ideas so that we do not stray far from the path as laid down by Zeno. Continuity and change is the nature of Existence. Likewise when it comes to the nature of Stoicism.

And if along the way we pique the interest of others and such helps them on their journey through life, all well and good. Hopefully such may enable them to feel more comfortable in their own faith. If however, for whatever reason, through reading both the writings of the ancient and the contemporary Stoics a person turns to Stoicism then that is to be their choice. The Stoic does not seek to overly convince others.

In restating Stoicism, we seek to ensure that our faith is maintained and kept relevant by looking to how advances in knowledge may reflect on some of our ideas. We seek to share in the duty that our faith lays on us, in that our faith tells us that it is our own individual responsibility to try to perform our roles in the play of life as best as we can while always trying 'to better our own personal best.'

A Stoic becomes a better Stoic by rationally and critically thinking about our Stoic beliefs. However, in such study it is the Stoic belief in the nature of the deity, the Stoic metaphysics and its many other interconnected principles that are the foundation that all issues are referred back to. In all issues we are guided to start from basics – seeing all as a Oneness, accepting 'what is' and appropriately striving in a manner that is in keeping with the actions of a person of good character. So when it comes down to it, a Stoic becomes a better Stoic by actually living in accord with their beliefs.

As an example of how a Stoic may see matters contrary to the popular view, from the Stoic perspective 'human rights' are the wrong way of looking at matters. 'Rights' are to lay responsibility on others 'to do what is necessary to respect one's rights', whereas the Stoic is encouraged to accept 'what is' and to see that if others do not offer 'due respect' such is something that is outside of our sphere of influence.

So the Stoic would not normally look to 'protecting their rights'.

What the Stoic has influence over is their own responsibilities to others, be it to individuals, society, the State, or even to animals, etcetera. Such responsibilities are governed by the Stoic's individual nature, their beliefs and their view of the ratio of responsibilities that their various roles in life demand of them – that is if they are to fulfil such roles to the best of their ability.

The Stoic may then, by extension, look to discussing the responsibilities that they may reasonably consider to be aspects of various roles in life – such as the responsibility of the State to its citizens, the responsibility of a business to its clients and so on. If the Stoic is in a position to influence such an attitude and policy in any of society's organisations, all well and good. It may then be that bodies and organisations within society can be influenced to move from that of looking to what 'rights' individuals have demanded to that of looking at and living up to their own responsibilities to those individuals and to society in general - such as their responsibility to pay their taxes to the State for the benefit of society as a whole without trying to be 'creative' in their avoidance of such taxes – where hopefully the State will live up to its responsibilities to care for the wellbeing of its citizenry and to govern society well and as is appropriate.

Looking at matters from the point of view of 'responsibilities' makes so much more sense than many demands for 'rights' do. In fact, demands for 'rights' are divisive and set people against people – often one group's 'rights' end up infringing another group's 'rights'. Whereas 'responsibility' is a cooperative matter in that every member of society, regardless of their role and status in life, may be seen as sharing in the responsibilities of society at all of its levels. Consideration is then given to what they, as individuals, bring to their roles by way of what they are responsible for as a result of those roles and what influence they may bring to bear and how they ought to share in any group responsibilities.

So much better to request that a person or organisation lives up to their responsibilities than to accuse them of 'trampling all over my rights'. The one asks them to live up to being a person of 'good character' or an organisation of 'good repute', while the other sets them up as being 'the enemy' and so drives them into a defensive position.

So much better to ask how they can help to solve a situation, than to accuse them of being the cause of the situation. If something has gone wrong, better to accept matters as they are and to seek cooperation in moving on.

All very Stoic in attitude.

As a result of applying the Stoic ways in this manner many issues will often be seen in a new light, especially if we look to the reality of the situation and accept the nature of 'what is' rather than trying to implement some intellectualised idealistic opinion as to 'how things ought to be'. Aiming for what is 'right and proper' through acceptance and appropriate striving is the Stoic way.

Looking to some popular issues, just as the Stoic will avoid looking to their 'rights', a Stoic will not demand 'equality' in that they know that no person is equal in every respect to any other person. We are all individuals.

After all, in certain respects no 'man' can be equal to a 'woman' in that he does not, by nature, have a womb. Their different physiology demands that they be treated differently – as and when such different treatment is appropriate. Also, Stoicism accepts that 'life is not fair'. Fate does not bestow on us all an equal share of the 'gifts of Fortune' – be it position, wealth, health or anything else. The Stoic looks to ensuring that they treat others in a just and appropriate manner for such is within their sphere of influence. We are grateful for whatever comes our way, be it bounty, sufficiency or dearth. But we do not expect or desire equality for such is something that is not fully within our sphere of influence.

When it comes to animal welfare, the Stoic will look to the fact that there is by nature a food-chain and that we are by nature omnivores. Eating or not eating meat is a matter of circumstance. It is not a moral issue. If it was, God would have made all animals vegetarians.

Those who live in the furthest northern reaches would have died out years ago if they did not eat meat, in that the climate allows for very little by way of vegetation. Most near-vegetarian diets are to be found closer to the equator where less energy is needed for keeping warm and only the occasional meat eating is needed in order to have a complete natural diet. I talk of 'near-vegetarian diets' in that the traditional diets of the world are rarely true vegetarian diets. Looking to arguments put forward by most vegetarian and vegan organisations, the arguments are often, in part, based on some intellectual misconception or on emotional consideration that talk of animal welfare, deforestation and other such issues.

Certainly, what matters when it comes to animal welfare is that we ensure that any hunting or farming of animals is done with care. The hunted animal ought to be dispatched as quickly as possible. Any farmed animal ought to be cared for appropriately so that they do not suffer unduly during their lifetime and their death ought to be as painless as is possible. But such is to be undertaken against the background that Nature has evolved us to eat meat as well as vegetation. A purely vegan diet sets us in thrall to 'big business' regards the need for dietary supplements, artificial fertilisers, etcetera.

We apply rationality to such matters. Arguments about how less land would be used if we all became vegans are false arguments. Some animals feed off land that is not appropriate for any other form of farming. The quality of the soil needed for growing many foods requires that the growing of vegetation for human consumption and the feeding of animals is rotated on the same land whereby the animal excrement provides the natural fertilisation and soil enhancement that is needed to grow the vegetation. To do otherwise, to grow only vegetation, would be to degrade our long-term ability to feed the population and also lead to whole species of farm animals having to be wiped out to provide the extra land needed for a purely vegan diet.

So in looking to what is rational, the Stoic is liable to see meat eating as a distraction, when the real issue regards depletion of the natural environment as farming expands is the number of humans on the planet

- it is not rational to try to find yet more ways to feed an ever growing population.

Population control is a natural stance for any Stoic. Nature tries her best. She produces a percentage of humans that are not able to reproduce. She produces a percentage of humans that are not attracted to their opposite sex so, in theory, reducing the number of couples who are liable to reproduce. She ensures that after a period of time our bodies degrade and we die. Yet we try to combat all of these controls. We try to go against Nature and look to IVF and other methods to provide children for those who were not born to have any. We hold onto life well beyond what ought to be our natural life span so not making way for the next generation. Like Zeno, we ought to be ready to leave life when Nature calls.

In all of these aspects Stoicism tells us that all is the individual's choice. However it also tells us, as individuals, to have consideration for the whole of society and not just look to our own selfish desires.

These are just some of the factors that a Stoic will look at. What decisions each Stoic may arrive at will be in accord with their overall individual beliefs and well thought out choices.

If one can live without causing harm to others so much the better. But one has to be clear as to what is meant by harm. If choosing not to eat meat means the extinction of the very farm animals that have been bred to be farm animals, the issue gets clouded. If every effort is to be made to bring as many children into the world as possible while also every effort is to be made to keep people alive as long as possible, we are working against Nature and not with her. 'Kindness' without thought can cause a conundrum.

So it is that Stoicism is not for everyone as the logic that its teachings lead to are not to the taste of all – even if the logic is sound and at times needs to be shouted from the rooftops.

The claim that Stoic thought relies on the Stoic belief in God and the Stoic metaphysics is not to say that non-Stoics cannot arrive at the same conclusions based on their beliefs. What it is to say is, that for the Stoic any conclusion they may arrive at is most likely to be correct if it does not contradict the overall Stoic view of life. Through our knowledge of the ever-present God that permeates the whole Cosmos, and the fact that we are one with our God, we are better able to stick to our principles and to follow a rational course through life that will be for the betterment of society – even when such may appear, to others, to be to our own individual detriment.

16. Effective Worrying

One of the main matters that holds a person back in partaking in the determinism that guides the flow of change for the better is unconstructive worrying.

One of the first practical teachings in Stoicism is regards ensuring that the 'impressions' we receive of the world about us are as true as possible to what is actually 'out there'. Such 'ensuring' requires that we 'choose' what we think is the correct 'impression'. On top of this we 'choose' what we think are the correct 'opinions' to hold about all and any subject (whether such 'opinions' are held at a conscious or subconscious level of thought), and then we 'choose' what action to take in response to the 'impressions' and our chosen 'opinions'.

Living life is an ongoing process of choice, be it choosing to accept matters as they are presented to us, choosing to try to influence how matters will progress, or choosing to accept and adapt to whatever the outcome is regards the influence or lack of influence of our earlier choices regards the flow of life – and then choosing to continue this whole process for as long as we live.

And when someone stops making effective choices? They become depressed – or worse.

It is known that to overcome many psychological issues, such as depression or addiction, the first step is always to make a choice – the choice that you are going to fight to get better. Without that initial choice to get better you will never step foot on the path to recovery.

At all of its levels, worrying is the state of not having made a necessary choice. It is the dithering that reflects the 'fight or flight' response where we are liable to agonise over which choice to make. And if we do not make a choice, we become stuck and make no progress.

Worrying is usually about a specific conscious choice that needs to be made.

However, while we worry, to some degree life goes on in that we are making all sorts of other choices all of the time. Every aspect of our bodily functions and activity, to some degree, involves choices at a subconscious level, and it has been shown that such can be affected by conscious choices – such as the ability to be able to lower one's blood pressure through contemplation. This is why our mental state affects our health and why, due to limitations being put on the range of choices we can make, ill health can affect our mental state.

We operate as 'single state individuals' in that every aspect of our being affects all the other aspects of our being. So while we can normally leave our subconscious to make many choices for us, when it comes to specific issues we need to ensure that we do not leave choices unmade – otherwise we will worry needlessly. And plain old simple worrying is no good for us.

We talk of a terrier dog as 'worrying' at a problem in that they keep working away until they solve the issue. To a great degree the Stoic training also guides us to work away until we solve any issue we are faced with.

We examine any 'impression' to ensure that it is true reflection of the situation. We examine our pre-existing 'opinions' to ensure that they are appropriate to the situation. We then select how to react to the situation.

All stages involve choice, but the one that will eliminate unproductive worrying is the 'final' choice to act – even if the action is to choose not to act until matters become clearer or because there is nothing to be done but to accept the situation as it is.

Being open to the fact that at all times, in all situations, we have a choice and that making a choice is the way to partake in determining how matters progress is the way to live in accord with Nature – and so to stop un-healthful worrying.

You may choose to seek out more information and so set a time by when the 'final' choice has to be made. In searching out the information you are worrying effectively in that you are acting according to your own choices – choices that you are in control of.

You may choose that matters will have to develop some more before you can make the next choice regards a situation. For instance, if you are waiting for input from someone else or from some official body, simply set a date in your calendar to chase them up if such is not forthcoming by that date and then stop worrying till then, in that there is nothing to be done in the meantime for you will have made a 'holding' choice and so can relax.

And when you are ready to make a 'final' choice to act, make it. But make it with the knowledge that you have done all that you can to ensure that the choice is based on what knowledge is available to you and in the knowledge that any action you may initiate may be thwarted and you may have to start all over again.

The Stoic is aware that no 'choice' is made in isolation. All choices relate to some situation or some aimed for outcome and, because of the fact that we live in a world that does not revolve around us as individuals, anything can happen that will require that we make new choices and so redirect our activities so as to stay in a state of harmony with Nature.

And for the Stoic, at all times, backing up our specific in the moment choices will be our primary choice, whereby we have chosen to follow the Stoic belief system and, as such, have chosen to try to be 'good people' – choices influencing choices.

All of which is why, for the Stoic, it is important to have a firm foundation of faith and purpose. A firm foundation is more likely to lead to sound judgements and sound choices. And as Epictetus guides us, in the end being 'good people' and doing what is appropriate all rests on the quality of our judgements and choices, and the quality of our judgements and choices rest on the quality of our principles and wisdom, where wisdom is the wise use of knowledge.

17. Looking at Mr or Mrs Perfect

All the talk of striving to emulate the actions of a sage is contrary to Zeno's wish to offer a philosophy of life that will benefit the person-in-the-street. Luckily enough Seneca presents us with the classic reasoned understanding of what Stoicism is offering.

'This is the mean of which I approve; our life should observe a happy medium between the ways of a sage and the ways of the world at large; all men should admire it, but they should understand it also.'
Seneca V. 'The Philosopher's Mean'

Many a person will have a low self-esteem. Some have an idea as to what they feel the qualities of the Mr. or Mrs. Perfect 'ought' to be and they feel that getting anywhere near to achieving such a target is next to impossible. In like manner, in Stoicism there is a risk that the concept of the nature of the 'sage' will have a similar effect on the Stoic student and so hold them back from putting all of their efforts into achieving their target of being a person that, for the most part, exhibits the good character that Stoicism trains us for.

As Seneca also tells us:

'Do you know why we have not the power to attain the Stoic Ideal? It is because we refuse to believe in our power. Nay, of a surety, there is something else which plays a part: it is because we are in love with our vices; we uphold them and prefer to make excuses for them rather than shake them off... The reason is unwillingness, the excuse, inability.'
Seneca CXVI. On Self Control

All too often the image of Mr. or Mrs. Perfect that we hold to is such that if we met such a perfect person they would most likely turn out to be quite unlikable. And those who try to act as they believe Mr. or Mrs. Perfect may act are liable to be missing the whole point by trying to be something they are not, especially as such efforts often involves using external objects, such as cars, home, furnishings and attire to create the imagined picture that they are trying to imitate.

Such striving after perfection often overlooks the fact that 'fineries' do not make someone a better person.

Far better to consider how an ordinary person of good character is liable to think and act. In this way one comes up with a person that is humane while still being just as liable to fall into error as we are - in that God has not made any one of us to be perfect beings.

We are designed in such a way that our senses may fool us, senses that are constantly having to come to terms with the ongoing flow of change that is Existence. There is no way that anyone can know all there is to know in order to make absolutely 'correct' judgements and to act in a manner that, in hindsight, will be seen to have been fully in harmony with Nature at all times. All that any person can hope for is that they act as best they can while accepting that, with time and experience, they will be more likely to act in a manner that actually does truly benefit the whole on a 'more often than not' basis.

When it comes down to it, we can reject any comparison with some irrational idealised image and simply recognise that all that is needed is to make the choice to set 'good character' and 'service to the whole' as one's ongoing target. Having done this one is actually already on the same road that a person of good character treads.

From then on, all that is needed is as constant an effort as one is able to muster whereby ongoing study, habituation and forethought add to one's resolve to follow the path one has chosen.

And of course, as with any journey, at times the journey through life will test our abilities but, in such testing, we will gain the wisdom to help us progress along the path. And with time we will become more skilful in how we cope with life's journey.

So there is no need to set some imagined out of reach ideal standard to aim for. All we need to aim for is completing the next step in the journey of life as best we can while being open to the steady improvement in our wisdom - whereby we will get better, day by day, at coping with whatever the flow of change throws at us.

The journey will last for the rest of our lives and each day is just another stage on that journey – right up to our last day. There will be no point at which sagehood is achieved. So better to be satisfied enough to be able to say 'I tried my best, and maybe tomorrow my best will be a little better.'

18. Reading the ancient Stoic texts

In reading the translations of the ancient texts we have need to be aware of two things. The influences (Christian, atheistic, etcetera) that affect the wording that the translator uses - and - the Greek and Roman cultures of the day and the influences such had on how they worded and presented matters (especially regards the idioms of the day and common understandings that did not, at the time, need to be stated in that, just as today, much is taken as common knowledge).

There are two particular areas of criticism that are often levelled at the Stoics of old that examples this point. Some critics claim that Stoicism sets women as being inferior to men and that Stoicism is prejudiced against homosexuals.

There is also criticism levelled at the Stoic view on suicide, which is sometimes seen as being detrimental regards mental health.

Stoicism on Women

Yes, throughout history there have been those who have a degrading opinion about the status of women, and Stoicism will not have been free of them. But the rationale of Stoicism regards the subject is summed up by Seneca in his letter 'To Marcia on Consolation' where he says:

'Who has asserted that Nature has dealt grudgingly with women's natures and has narrowly restricted their virtues? Believe me, they have just as much force, just as much capacity, if they like, for virtuous action; they are just as able to endure suffering and toil when they are accustomed to them.'

As is the case for the males of the species.

No doubt if someone is looking for wording that appears to contradict this, they will find something to latch onto. However, in true Stoic fashion one needs to ask as to if words have the power to hurt oneself, or is it one's opinions about the words that is causing any hurt.

As the child's quote so Stoically says: 'Sticks and stones may break my bones, but words will never hurt me.'

For instance, the much-vaunted claim that Stoicism suggests that 'women are the common property of men'.

By looking carefully, using the Stoic rationale as a guide, it may be seen that the intent of what was written differs to how the words may appear to our modern minds. As Seneca advises, look to the intent of what is being said, not the individual words.

What was written was written in a time when many a husband did not return from the wars and, with no welfare state, it was seen to be the common responsibility of the surviving males to offer protection and support to the family of the dead while also respecting women in general.

Within Stoicism, 'common property' in no way was meant to suggest that a man could go with any woman that he wanted. Exclusivity in relationships, such as through marriage, was recognised as needing to be honoured. Which is why, generally, adultery was seen as being against Nature. And of course, this exclusivity was a two-way street – the man and the woman were both expected to honour the marriage contract until such time as one or the other acted in a manner that voided it or they mutually agreed to end the 'contract'.

As to terminology, much in the extant Stoic writings refer to being a man and to manliness. This was in part due to the fact that much of the discussions that have come down to us originated in symposiums and the like where, due to the culture of the day, only men were present and so the discussion centred around the male point of view. But it may also be put down to the fact that, as is to be recognised by any reasoning person, for millennia, where talking of 'man', as appropriate, 'man' is to be taken to referring to all of humankind.

So it is, according to context, where the writings talk generally about 'man', they are also talking of 'women' where, for example, the subject matter applies to all of the human species.

As to the translation 'manliness', because of today's sometimes derisory connotations surrounding the term 'womanliness', it is better to see the term 'manliness' as referring to the Stoic call for all people to act as people of good character who live wisely, justly, courageously and with moderation – be they male or female.

It may also be seen that, in many respects, males of the human species are to be seen as nothing more than being of mankind, whereas females are recognised as holding a special position, in that they are the child bearers.

Even Nature confirms this, in that females have evolved to have two X chromosomes, whereas the male has only one X chromosome and the far punier Y chromosome, whereby Nature has given the female a stronger immune system than the male, so favouring the female when faced with the diseases that Nature throws at us, etcetera. Nature sees a greater need for the survival of females so as to ensure the survival of the next generation.

As such, the males, that were not killed off in battle or by disease, were seen to be there to support and protect all the females and their children as and when necessary.

While men and women are never going to be equal in that a male does not give birth to children, in all other respects Stoic rationale tells us that males and females are of equal status.

Confirming this, while many cultures had evolved traditions whereby marriage had become mostly about a contract between two families where the woman was effectively offered as 'a bond' to seal the contract, Stoicism saw marriage as the voluntary coming together of two 'soul-mates' whereby both parties saw marriage as 'two souls becoming one soul' where the marriage contract is that of two equals who marry because of what they see in the other person. In the Stoic marriage there is no imbalance of power or status. It is solely a commitment between two people to faithfully share their journey through life for as long as the marriage exists. The Stoic marriage is not entered into in order to benefit family or business or any other 'external' purpose.

And of course, as with any contract, a marriage is seen as ending as and when one partner within the marriage acts adulterously or in any other way abuses the marriage contract. Otherwise, the marriage ends with the death of one of the spouses or when both parties mutually agree that the contract has run its course. The Stoic marriage exists through trust, mutual respect and agreement.

So, following the Stoic rationale, in Stoicism a person is only superior to another regards specific skills, such as one person being superior to another in their running skills. There is nothing to say that a person, man or woman, has overall superiority to any other person – especially as we are all manifested out of the body of God.

Which is why the Stoic rationale does not discriminate between people on the grounds of sex or race, etcetera.

Stoicism on Homosexuality

In similar vein, at times we are told that Rufus Musonius said that homosexuality is 'contrary to Nature'. However, the full quote is:

"But of all sexual relations those involving adultery are most unlawful, and no more tolerable are those of men with men, because it is a monstrous thing and contrary to nature"
Lecture XII, On sexual indulgence.

If read correctly and within context, this reads as saying that: "adultery is a monstrous thing and contrary to nature", in that any extra-marital relationship is a breach of the faithfulness that the marriage contract has promised – regardless of the sex of the 'other person' or if the marriage is between a same-sex couple. Stoicism says that a marriage contract is between two people only, whereby the one-to-one faithfulness that is commonly expected to occur within a marriage ought not to be damaged.

It does not say that "men with men" (or "women with women"), where adultery is not being committed, is 'contrary to Nature', only that adultery is 'contrary to Nature' because to enter into a marriage and to then be unfaithful makes the person less than they ought to be - in that they are not acting as a person of good character would.

To try to provide yet more supposed 'evidence' of homophobia within Stoicism, some quote Seneca and his Moral Letters 122.7 as 'evidence' of such:

Do you not believe that men live contrary to Nature who exchange the fashion of their attire with women? Do not men live contrary to Nature who endeavour to look fresh and boyish at an age unsuitable for such an attempt? What could be more cruel or more wretched? Cannot time and man's estate ever carry such a person beyond an artificial boyhood?

We are in fact told that the reference to 'exchanging the fashion' actually refers to the wearing of silk and transparent fabrics, which in those days was seen as being a sign of a man being overly self-indulgent, akin with people who try to hide their age by trying to retain 'the look of youth' – as against accepting the natural process of aging.

This, after all, is followed by:

Do not men live contrary to Nature who crave roses in winter, or seek to raise a spring flower like the lily by means of hot-water heaters and artificial changes of temperature? Do not men live contrary to Nature who grow fruit- trees on the top of a wall? Or raise waving forests upon the roofs and battlements of their houses - the roots starting at a point, to which it would be outlandish for the tree-tops to reach? Do not men live contrary to Nature who lay the foundations of bathrooms in the sea and do not imagine that they can enjoy their swim unless the heated pool is lashed as with the waves of a storm?

All aspects of decrying attempts to ignore the true nature of things. It is not about people being born homosexual.

We are again pointed to Seneca's Natural Questions 1.16.1, reporting the actions of Hostius Quadra as an example of the supposed prejudice against homosexuals:

There was a man called Hostius Quadra, whose obscenity was even the subject of a stage performance. The divine Augustus

considered this rich and greedy man, a slave to his millions,
unworthy of vengeance when he was murdered by his slaves,
and almost pronounced he seemed to have been killed
lawfully. He was not depraved only with one sex, but was as
greedy for men as for women, and made mirrors of the kind I
mentioned above which reflect much bigger images, in which
fingers exceed the length and width of arms. He arranged
these in such a way that when he himself was enduring a man,
he could see behind him all the movements of his stallion and
enjoy the false length of his own member as if it were true.

Yet here the object of Seneca's derision is the man's propensity for obscenity and depravity in that Hostius Quadra was quite clearly seen to sexually abuse both men and women – which is probably the reason that people tolerated the fact that his slaves murdered him. Their actions were probably seen as being that of self-defence.

Again, not a judgement regards homosexuals, but rather a critique of those who abuse others for their own perverse pleasure – regardless of their sexual nature.

There will have been individuals identified as Stoics who were prejudiced against homosexuals, as there have always been throughout all ages and societies, despite the fact that the Stoic rationale allows for no such prejudice.

What matters in Stoicism is not who or what a person is, but how they act in relation to all about them. And how does Stoicism guide each individual to act? In accord with Nature and with wisdom, justice, courage, and moderation.

Suicide

The Stoic view on dying at the time of one's choosing is complex. Compare the following statements by Seneca:

'Mere living is not a good, but living well. Accordingly the wise man will live as long as he ought, not as long as he can.'
'This is one reason why we cannot complain of life: it keeps no one against his will.'
Seneca On the Proper Time to Slip the Cable LXX.

'One must indulge genuine emotions; sometimes, even in spite of weighty reasons, the breath of life must be called back and kept at our very lips even at the price of great suffering, for the sake of those whom we hold dear; because the good man should not live as long as it pleases him, but as long as he ought. He who does not value his wife, or his friend, highly enough to linger longer in life – he who obstinately persists in dying – is a voluptuary.'
Seneca On the Care of Health and Peace of Mind CIV.

'Do you ask what is the highway to liberty? Any vein in your body.'
Seneca On Anger III.xvi.

'O Life, by the favour of Death I hold thee dear!'
Seneca To Marcia on Consolation xx

'Most men ebb and flow in wretchedness between the fear of death and the hardships of life; they are unwilling to live, and yet they do not know how to die.'
Seneca On the Terrors of Death IV

Life is not incomplete if it is honourable. At whatever point you leave off living, provided you leave off nobly, your life is a whole.
It is with life as it is with a play, it matters not how long the action is spun out, but how good the acting is. It makes no difference at what point you stop. Stop whenever you choose; only see to it that the closing period is well turned.
Seneca On Taking One's Own LIfe LXXVII.

'We need to be warned and strengthened in both directions, not to love or to hate overmuch; even when reason advises us to make an end of it, the impulse is not to be adopted without reflection or at headlong speed. The brave and wise man should not beat a hasty retreat from life; he should make a becoming exit. '
Seneca On Despising Death XXIV.

Stoics are taught to make the most of their life because death is a certainty. The timing of death may be sudden and unexpected or it may be expected imminently as a result of a lingering illness or the like. But death will come to all of us.

So, for the Stoic, death is a reality of life and is not to be feared, in that it is to be accepted as part of 'living in accord with Nature'.

Due to the nature of Fate, death may come at any time. Stoicism tells us that knowing this will help us to make the most of the present moment that we are living, while always encouraging us to keep an eye on planning for the future – in case we live through to tomorrow. We need to live providently – that is, with forethought – as part of living for the whole.

However, in that we are possessed of a freewill, for the Stoic, death at a time of their own choosing is always an option - if fate does not step in first.

One reason a Stoic may choose to die is if the choice is between dying honourably or living dishonourably. Fortunately, there are few situations where the choice is so stark. Wise consideration will nearly always find an alternate path that will allow one to live life honourably.

So it is that Stoicism recognises that where a person looks to ending their own life, they need to take great care so as to ensure that they are acting wisely and not out of desperation. The greater good generally overrides any selfish wish to avoid the suffering that living may impose.

To commit suicide in a fit of despair is liable to cause harm to friends and loved ones. However, Stoicism looks favourably on suicide that aims to reduce ongoing suffering, provided such is done in a manner and for reasons that friends and loved ones can understand and, hopefully, approve of. A Stoic will apply wisdom, reasoning and rationalism, rather than emotional influences, when considering a wish to commit suicide, while recognising that each case will have its own individual circumstance and circle of influence that need to be taken into consideration.

And one of the first bits of wisdom to consider for a person wishing to commit suicide is that they take steps to ensure that the 'wish' is not that of an 'unsound mind'. In this day and age, where possible and as appropriate, Stoicism would recommend that professional medical help is sought so as to ensure that a mental or physical illness is not affecting one's ability to reason rationally and wisely.

All of the above examples show that we need to take an overview of the ancient Stoic texts and so see any matter in the context of the overall

Stoic rationale so as to better understand what is being said, while also seeing past any individual's opinion, comment or turn of phrase that runs contrary to the 'big picture'.

19. Socrates' 'Divine Something' considered against the rationale of Zeno's Metaphysics

This supposed rejection by Stoicism of what Professor Gilbert Murray calls 'magical powers or supernatural knowledge' in his 1915 lecture is a popular idea in today's modern world. However, when looking to the rationale of the Stoic metaphysics there is much that is today disparagingly called 'supernatural' that is to be seen as being 'natural' when considering the Stoic worldview.

Many people from all over the world, from all eras, have reported how they have benefited from 'divine guidance' in some form or other. As an example of such 'divine guidance', from Socrates we have:

"You have often times and in many places heard me give –
that there comes to me a something divine and spiritual, which
Meletus indeed, by way of a joke, has included in his
indictment; and this is a voice which since childhood has
frequently come to me, and which makes itself heard only to
turn me back from what I am about to do, but never to impel
me forward.
Socrates' Apology

With Socrates being held up as such a key figure in Western philosophy and being the inspiration for what is often called the Socratic Method of critical thinking, which is very much the forerunner of the 'scientific method', it is difficult for many a 'modern' to accept this aspect of Socrates' life. Here is 'the great man' offering an insight into a very personal relationship with God – a situation that many would rather not admit to, to the extent that it is often suggested that Socrates did not really mean what he said.

But if Socrates did not mean what he said then he would have been going against all that he believed regards straight talking and honesty. The nature of his death would have been in vain if, in this area, he was stating matters to be other than as he genuinely believed them to be. Based on his reputation we have to accept that Socrates was stating matters truthfully when he talked of receiving guidance from his 'divine something' or 'daimonion'.

Now the Stoics of old looked into such matters and, believing that 'a spark of God' is part of our very being, they saw that individuals ought to be able to 'commune' with other aspects of the living Cosmos – aspects that are 'more than' just the 'spark' of 'the Consciousness'/God that permeates our own individualised body.

We are talking of something that may be seen as being akin to the World Wide Web. We are talking of a 'Cosmos Wide Network of Consciousness' where one can garner 'information' from a greater pool of consciousness than is possible through our own normally recognised individual senses and experiences. We are in effect talking of what is sometimes called extrasensory perception. But being that we are talking of Stoicism, the 'Consciousness' is physical in nature in that the 'active principle' is as physical as the 'passive principle'. As such we are not talking of 'extrasensory' but, according to the Stoic rationale, we are talking of the sensory experience that is Reason/Rationality. To the followers of Stoicism 'the reasoning faculty' is a sixth physical faculty on a par with touch, sight, hearing, taste and smell whereby through Reason/Rationality we can better experience 'the true reality' of the world about us.

The reasoning faculty is the sense that 'sees' the rationale of the 'information' that the other senses are providing us with.

The reasoning faculty; for this is the only one we have
inherited which will take knowledge both of itself - what it is,

and of what it is capable, and how valuable a gift it is to us -
and likewise of all the other faculties.
Epictetus

And in looking to Socrates and other such cases, the Stoic of old concluded that this sixth sense allows us, at times, to commune with the 'Reason' and 'Rationality' that permeates the Cosmos.

Following the Stoic rationale that stems from the Stoic view of the nature of the Cosmos, such access to a wider pool of 'information' is not to be seen as supernatural, but merely as a natural consequence of the nature of the Cosmos and how it is made manifest.

Indeed, no man can be good without the help of God. ... He it
is that gives noble and upright counsel.'
Seneca On the God Within Us XLI

'One God immanent in all things,... and one Law, one Reason
common to all intelligent creatures, and one Truth.'
Marcus Aurelius VII.9

Looking to the Stoic metaphysics whereby the whole Cosmos is permeated by a single 'Consciousness', it is rational to see that this 'Consciousness' also permeates us as individuals. So God, the 'active principle' of the Stoic prime matter, also provides a channel for a 'conscious' communication between us and all else within the Cosmos. How this works and what limits and filters our nature as animals puts on our ability to 'commune' with the rest of the Cosmos is open to question, but it is a question I have had a personal interest in.

Quite clearly we are not designed to be open to the whole spectrum of the 'Consciousness' that is God. The way we are designed we are clearly not able to cope with all the 'information' that is available within the Cosmos as a whole. But separate to our five physical senses there are aspects of this pool of 'information' that we are open to, mostly at a subconscious level, with such communication occasionally coming to the attention of our conscious state as 'telepathy', 'empathy', 'prescience' and answers to prayers etcetera.

Many people today with a scientific leaning tend to ridicule such ideas in that the experiences we are talking of here are individualistic, experiential in the moment and are not normally repeatable and so they cannot be subjected to scientific examination through the 'scientific method'. The fact that science cannot get to grips with such sixth sense events is not surprising in that science has still not got to grips with what 'Consciousness' is, so science is unlikely to be able to come to grips with aspects of how Consciousness/God 'operates', especially when it comes to the individual's experiences of being in communication with 'Something' that has access to a wider spectrum of the Consciousness that permeates the Cosmos than is normal for the individual human when it comes to daily life.

But despite such ridicule, people all around the world still today believe in such matters. In fact, when asked, all but the determined atheist will admit to some experience in their lives that could be explained by an understanding of the Stoic rationale that is led by the Stoic metaphysics. Telepathic moments, the feelings of the presence of loved ones who have died, the comfort that comes with feelings of being 'hugged' by 'Another' and the feelings of being guided by some 'higher being' – all of these and more are common experiences of humankind. For those for whom being consciously aware of such experiences are infrequent, it is easy for them to brush such aside as some 'glitch' in their thought processes. But taken as a whole, the statistics relating to the reported occurrences of sixth sense experiences across the world gives credence to the reality of such experiences and such personal experiences is what often holds a person to their faith regardless of the onslaught of the atheistic attempts to deride religions and the like.

However, looking back to one aspect of the quote from Socrates, he states that his 'divine something' 'makes itself heard only to turn me back from what I am about to do, but never to impel me forward.' We do have to be careful that any acceptance of such sixth sense 'information' as being appropriate is in keeping with the Stoic aim to live as a person of good character.

While we may get guidance as Socrates did from a 'divine something', by the nature of the universality of the Consciousness it is possible that we may get 'input of information' that seems to be guiding us to acts that are contrary to 'those things which the common law of mankind is in the habit of forbidding'. Such negative 'input' will be the result of the internal workings of an unsound mind or the result of empathic fallout from the minds of others who are of unsound mind.

Such 'information' from unsound minds tends to try to impel a person towards some antisocial action of other. Whereas 'sixth sense information' from a 'divine something' tends to guide against unsound action or it may offer access to a wider pool of 'information' to better help the individual to try to determine their own course of action for themselves.

Stoic rationale tells us that we are possessed of a freewill, gifted to us by God. So it is unlikely, from the Stoic point of view, that any divine 'inner voices' or the like would drive us towards action that would be contrary to our freewill where, as Stoics, we have chosen to try to manifest our actions in a manner whereby others will see them as being 'in accord with Nature' while also being the actions of a person of good character.

As with many things in life, Stoicism throws up apparent contradictions. And this subject matter is no different. Stoic metaphysics offers us the concept of everything being manifestations of 'a singular state of being', yet at the same time we also recognise individualities within that Oneness. So we are both one with the Whole and at the same time we are separated by the nature of our being individual members of a species of animal. Because of our nature we experience ourselves as having an individual identity whereby we experience our 'self' as being separate from everything else and as such everything else is seen at some level as being 'external' to our 'self'.

While much about living the Stoic life requires us to recognise that we are manifested out of the body of God and so are one with all around us, our nature and some of the Stoic training looks to aspects of existence as 'externals'. So while 'God is within us' in that we are manifested out of the passive and active principles of the prime matter that is the body of God, so also we experience God as being 'something else' whereby, for instance, Socrates experiences the 'voice' of his 'divine something' as 'coming to him'. He recognises this 'voice' as being something other than the outpourings of his own mind. He recognises the 'voice' as being from 'Something' with a greater 'knowledge' of events as they are unfolding than he did and so Socrates also recognises that the 'voice' was able to manifest a greater wisdom than Socrates could in that Socrates had less knowledge to work with.

In Stoicism, God is 'the all and the everything' and so God, as the Cosmos, has access to all knowledge/information. We as individual animals are limited in our access to 'information' and so have to do our best with what 'information' we have available to us through the limitations of our senses. But every now and then, through our sixth sense, as individuals we are presented with guidance from 'Something' that is greater than our own individual nature – 'Something' that is able to help and guide us in that It has access to more of the spectrum of 'information' than we do.

Our minds may see such 'Somethings' as being Daemons (aspects of God), Angels, the spirits of dead ancestors or something else seen as 'divine somethings'. Stoicism avoids such debate about the nature of what it is that will at times 'guide' us to making wiser choices. We see all as being 'of God'. A bit like a Company that has many divisions and many workers in the many divisions. When we are contacted by or try to contact the Company it is not our concern which division or which individual deals with our communications for they are all part of the one organisation. We communicate with the Company and how the Company communicates with us is up to it. So also is the Stoic view of any communion with God.

Epictetus, in keeping with the Stoic rationale, guides us to make our will one with the will of God. Stoicism tells us that generally we can know what it is best to try to determine in life by looking to what God is manifesting all around us. That is, by looking to the bigger picture of all that is around us we can learn how we can best fit into the play of life. Which is why, in aligning our individual will with the will of God, the Stoic guidance is 'to live in accord with Nature'. But that being said, history tells us that on occasions 'Something' will step in and help guide us towards the better.

20. On Fate, Foreknowledge and Divination

The future is not preordained. It is not already mapped out in totality as a result of the physical laws of cause and effect.

Yet the Stoics of old believed in the practicality of divination – and what else does divination do than state what the future holds in store for us? Well actually it does not. All that divination does is to forecast what is liable to happen based on present circumstances. The purpose of consulting an 'oracle' was to get a little help in planning ahead. It was not to find out what was inevitable – what Stoic would go out of their way to find out about the inevitable, when they would find out about it in the fullness of time. The reason for trying to find out something about the future has to be in order to try to do something to improve one's lot in the face of what is liable to happen.

After all, Stoic training tells us to plan for possible future scenarios so that we will be better prepared to face up to them. Even without an 'Oracle', we can predict possible futures for ourselves.

The Stoics of old did not believe that the future was totally preordained and that their only choice in life was between acceptance of the life they were faced with and that of increasing their suffering by mentally fighting against the inevitable. They went to all the trouble of investigating life and formulating a philosophy in the certainty that wisdom would not only help them cope with what they had no control over, but would also help them to influence matters towards the better where they did have some influence.

A car driver wishing to stop their car knows that if they wish to stop at a point they need to start applying their brakes some time before arriving at that point – they rely on predicting the future. They know that if they arrive at the point without having planned ahead that there is no way they would be able to stop instantly – that is unless the point happens to be a very strong wall. However, having planned to stop at the point, and despite taking the necessary action to apply their brakes in the correct manner there is much that can go wrong. In this case, maybe an earlier bit of divination might have helped – especially if it was able to warn one that one really should get one's brakes fixed, so helping one to avoid the accident that is liable to occur when one overshoots the point through faulty brakes.

The idea that a wise enough person would be able to predict what the future holds if they knew all there was to know about this instant only works regards matters that are only ruled by 'physical' laws. When there is 'a spark of the Divine Fire' involved there is no such certainty. It may be possible to predict in a limited way the reactions of a person to a given situation if one knows enough about the person, but over time it would not be possible to predict their every action – their freewill allows them to choose their reaction, and often their actions within any given situation. And while they may, out of habit, normally choose a particular path, on a whim they may just happen to choose to step out of character and do something just because they want to, so confounding any prediction as to their actions.

With enough knowledge and understanding it might be possible to predict an earthquake, but it is not possible to predict with any degree of certainty just how everyone will react to it. One person makes one choice and they die. If they make another choice they live. To turn left or right? There is no indication as to which is the better choice! One turns left, and one dies. Replay this. One turns right, and one lives.

The earthquake is inevitable (always provided some vast rock travelling through space does not smash the planet to bits a moment earlier). Death lies round one corner, life round the other, and it is only a matter of whim that decides which turn the person takes. Until they make their choice the probability regards their future is on hold – it could go either way. They make the choice…..

And it is this power of choice that we Stoics clearly state is within our control – a gift from the Deity, our reasoning faculty that is a spark of the Divine Fire.

What is not within our full control is the result of our choices, as so much else is happening over which we have no control. However for us to have control over our choices, so also we must have a 'Producer' of the 'Play of Life' that allows us to adlib. And as we adlib so the 'Playwright' has to adapt the 'play' to accommodate our adlibbing.

From the Stoic point of view, Fate may be viewed as the design limitations of the Cosmos within which we find ourselves. From the moment the car brakes are applied it is fate that it must travel on further before stopping.

The future is just a probability based on what has gone before and the various influences that may come to bear in the Now by way of our using the spark of Divine Fire that has been allocated to us. There is no way a Stoic would accept that the Future is totally preordained.

As to Foreknowledge, this ought more to be referred to as prediction based on what is, rather than knowledge as to what is to be. The diviner, if they have any true ability, at times taps into a wider spectrum of the Divine Fire than is normal for an individual, and acquires a greater awareness of the flow of events and where such might lead. They will acquire 'knowledge' that is not available to them in the normal course of events. However, the diviner is not necessarily able to apply their gift at will, and will often be tempted to make things up as they go along in order to give the 'client' their money's worth. In addition, even when they have 'seen' the probabilities in store, they are liable to colour the information they pass on to their 'client' with their own hang ups and opinions. All of which is why seeking the guidance of a diviner is a very risky business.

The best foreknowledge for a Stoic is achieved through the 'right use of knowledge'/wisdom. The Stoic will base all of their actions in the Now on such, aiming for what their foreknowledge (prediction of the probable future) tells them is the best course, while being ready to accept whatever happens should their actions miss the mark due to something of which they are unaware or over which they have no control.

The Stoic accepts what is Fated, but is ready to harmonise with the Cosmos and work towards the better. They will try to influence future events where appropriate; they will not just passively accept them without question.

21. Restating Stoicism – not reinventing it

My writings tend to meet with objections because of the way I express matters. While we are told by Seneca that each Stoic needs to bring a piece of themselves to their understanding of what Stoicism involves, I speak and write with a certainty that others are sometimes uncomfortable with.

Following on from my experiences of something akin to Socrates' daimonion I have a certainty about the immanence of God as understood by Stoicism.

As a result, I also have a certainty about the soundness of the Stoic metaphysics in that, through looking to what the world faiths and what the modern sciences tell us, I arrived at my understanding of the 'three prime dimensions' of Space, Movement and Consciousness that are aspects of the processes behind the manifestation of the Cosmos – only to be led to a book on Stoicism where I discovered that Zeno had been there before me. I found that I had rediscovered Stoicism's metaphysics including its belief that the prime dimension of Consciousness (the active principle) is to be equated with the realisation that God permeates the whole Cosmos, albeit that I was restating the Stoic metaphysics in light of the advances in knowledge up to today's times.

This certainty leads me to agree with the classic Stoic stance that Stoicism offers us a complete guide to living life if, and only if, we buy into its faith and metaphysics, in that this is the foundation to the Stoic mantra 'to live in accord with Nature' where, according to Stoicism, Nature is the oneness that is the living Cosmos, the body of God, out of which we and all around us are manifested.

It is no coincidence that the modern use in Stoicism of the word Nature with a capital 'N' is a translation of the Greek 'Phusis' which is the root from which our modern word 'physics' comes. For the Stoics, 'Phusis' is Nature seen as the living evolving state that is forever being manifested here and now by God and it is only through looking to what God is manifesting that we can learn how to live.

As such, Nature, Phusis or the physics of life is what is behind the rationale that leads to the Stoic ethics – where 'ethics' relates to the 'ethos' of the Stoic. That is, the 'nature, disposition and habituated customs' of an individual that understands their place in the scheme of things. The Stoic ethics is about how the Stoic will live, where such is based on the Stoic faith, metaphysics and the nature of the Existence which we find all around us.

As a result of all of the above I go against the modern trend of trying to extract parts of the Stoic training and calling it Stoicism. I hold to the classic Stoic stance that says Stoicism is a complete whole, where its understanding of Nature ('Phusis'), its consequential rationale and its ethos are one.

Along with the Stoics of old, today's renowned experts in the study of Stoicism confirm the classic Stoic take that the ethos of the Stoic is to be firmly grounded in the Stoic faith in an imminent and providential God that is manifesting the world about us, moment by moment. And Epictetus could be no clearer – the Stoic's ethos is to align their will with the will of God.

So I hold to the classic Stoic principle that the edifice that is Stoicism will not stand unless its three pillars (its physics, its rationale and its ethics) are all in place. Remove one and the edifice falls.

This may make me a 'fundamentalist' in some people's eyes, but such also makes Seneca, Epictetus and Marcus Aurelius 'fundamentalists' in that they all followed the fundamentals of Stoicism.

So, in my view of Stoicism I try to stay true to the rationale of the classic Stoicism as originally introduced by Zeno. I also try to consider such against the advances in knowledge since Zeno's time, while often finding much in modern thinking that supports and confirms the Stoic stance on many issues.

In looking to the Stoic principles afresh, starting with the basics and adding in the new knowledge and ways of describing and expressing things today, I find it sensible to try to offer a new conversation on how we can describe and explain many of the Stoic ideas in a manner that will be more understandable to the populous today.

This may offend many who want to hold to certain ways of saying things as has become the 'orthodoxy' of today. However, in his day, Zeno offered a teaching that was meant to be suitable for the person-in-the-street. Matters became more complicated and technical as Zeno and his followers tried to explain their ideas to the more intellectual schools in Athens and so we ended up with all sorts of technical terminology and logical arguments that make Stoicism appear, in places, to be counter-intuitive, dogmatic and the province of an elite.

I aim to try to talk non-technically about the whole nature of Stoicism, including its metaphysics and its reliance on understanding the nature of life. I aim to take the rationale of the classic Stoic beliefs and wisdom and to state such anew in order to maintain an understanding of how we ought, as Stoics, to habituate ourselves regards trying to live a life of 'good' whereby we 'live in accord with Nature' in all of its guises. And here the act of habituating ourselves is what is meant by 'ethics' – the Stoic ethics often being seen as the prime interest of many a would-be-Stoic.

However, in being true to Zeno and classic Stoicism, it is a Stoic principle that our ethos, our habituated way of acting, is dependent on our understanding of the physics of life – both the nature of the life we are living here on Earth and the nature of our relationship to the Cosmos as a whole, a Cosmos that is the body of God. This is all part of the Stoic rationale that ties the Stoic ethics firmly to the Stoic physics.

The rationale of Stoicism means that the Stoic mind training, that is often taken to be all there is to the 'ethics', is not the Stoic 'ethics' if taken in isolation. To have a chance of understanding Stoicism, just as was the case two millennia ago, one needs to gain an understating of the physics of life as Stoicism sees it. The Stoic ethics are only to be perceived through an understanding of the Stoic physics and metaphysics.

Just as Cognitive Behavioural Therapy (CBT) is grounded in similar mind training as is on offer in the Stoic teachings, it is to be applauded if the Stoic mind training helps an individual to better cope with life. However, to be a Stoic of the classic vein, to be a Stoic that walks side by side with Zeno, Seneca, Epictetus, Marcus Aurelius and the other Stoics of old, requires immersion in the whole of Stoicism - the physics, the rationale and the ethos. It requires a belief in the Stoic understanding of the nature of the Cosmos and the God that manifests it as the body of God.

22. Other Views and Readings

I have offered a view of Stoicism that is simple and is based on the classic Stoic theistic view of the nature of the existence we find ourselves living in. To repeat the quote from Marcus Aurelius:

Constantly think of the universe as one living creature,
embracing one being and soul; how all is absorbed into the
one consciousness of this living creature; how it compasses all
things with a single purpose, and how all things work together
to cause all that comes to pass, and their wonderful web and
texture.
Marcus Aurelius

By referencing all of one's choices in life back to this and the other Stoic principles one will be guided to live selflessly in service to all that exists about us – in accord with the Stoic way.

Living as a Stoic is the way to be a Stoic. With practice and forethought, the practicalities of living as a Stoic will become habit. Naturally the more one understands the Stoic way the easier it will become to live as a Stoic.

What I have written is my view of Stoic thought – a view that I believe Zeno would recognise. My nature and my experiences will have coloured how I present it. So for those who wish to study more and to get other opinions, I would suggest the following reading in that these present the understanding of classic Stoicism as a whole sphere of thought.

The classical writings offer the opinions of other Stoics, but one needs to be careful regards the translations in that different translators can at times word matters according to their own beliefs. One also needs to be aware of the social climate of the time of the early Stoics and the limitations of the Greek theorising regards matters scientific. Like today, their observation was far more reliable than their theory.

The commentaries offer the study of classical Stoicism and are mostly the result of the study of Stoicism by academic professors who are looking at Stoicism in its historic context and are not approaching the subject as Stoics. But even here the academics still tend to colour their presentation with their own personal worldview.

Stoic Classical Writings

The Loeb Classical Library. (Excellent English translations accompanied by the Greek or Latin texts.)

'Seneca Epistles Morales' Translation by Richard M Gummere. LCL volumes 75, 76 & 77.

'Seneca Moral Essays' Translation by John W Basore. LCL volumes 214, 254 and 310.

'Epictetus, the discourses as reported by Arrian, the Manual and Fragments' Translated by W A Oldfather. LCL volumes 131 & 218.

'The Communings with Himself of Marcus Aurelius Antoninus, together with his speeches and essays' Translated by C R Haines. LCL volume 58.

'Lives of Eminent Philosophers' Diogenes Laertius Volume II (Book VII) – Translated by R D Hicks. LCL volume 185

Other Sources

'Musonius Rufus – the Roman Socrates' by Cora Lutz 1947 Yale Classic Studies Volume X, Yale University Press

Cicero's 'De Officiis' and his 'The Tusculan Disputations' and other writings.

'Greek and Roman Philosophy After Aristotle' Edited by Jason L Saunders. Published by The Free Press, New York and Collier MacMillan Ltd, London. 1966 (Of interest for a collection of fragments relating to Stoicism)

Commentaries etc.

'Encyclopaedia Britannica -15th Edition 2002, 'Philosophical Schools & Doctrines - Stoicism', Macropaedia Book 25 (commentary by Jason L Saunders); and 'Stoicism', Micropaedia Book 11. (Excellent summaries of various aspects of Stoic philosophy and historical background of the Stoas. Information on other aspects of Stoicism and the major figures involved may be found using the index to access the many references to Stoicism.)

'The Stoic Philosophy' Gilbert Murray. The 1915 Conway Memorial Lecture. Published by Watts & Co 1918; also in 'Essays and Addresses' published by Allan & Unwin, 1921. (An excellent short professorial summary of Stoicism by a 'non-believer' – well worth the read if you can obtain a copy.)

'Stoic Studies' A A Long. Published by Cambridge University Press. 1996

'Hellenistic Philosophy' A A Long. Published by Duckworth, London. 1974.

'Roman Stoicism' E V Arnold. Published by Cambridge Press. 1911 republished 1958.

'Stoic Philosophy' J M Rist. Published by Cambridge University Press. 1969, republished 1980.

'Stoicism and its Influence' R M Wenley. Published by Marshal Jones, Boston – 1924, Harrap, London – 1925.

'Stoics and Sceptics' Edwyn Beven. Published by Oxford Press. 1913.

'The Meaning of Stoicism' Ludwig Edelstein. The Martin Lecture Series. Published for Oberlin College by Harvard University Press. 1966.

'The Philosophy Of Chrysippus' Josiah B Gould. Published by E J Brill, Leiden. 1970.

'The Stoics' F H Sandbach. Published by Chatto & Windus. 1975.

23. Two schools of Stoicism in the 21st Century

In the late twentieth/early twenty-first century there has been a renewed interest in the Stoic teachings and, while understanding and following Stoicism is very much an individual journey, two new schools have come into being. These are Modern Stoicism and Traditional Stoicism.

These two schools have some subtle and not so subtle differences in their aims and understandings.

So, to look at the two modern day schools:

Modern Stoicism
This school coalesced as a result of a discussion by academics and psychotherapists that was held at the University of Exeter over the two days of 5th and 6th of October 2012. The aim was to see if Stoic training could be used to add to the work being done through Cognitive Behavioural Therapy and other similar therapeutic disciplines.

Out of this came the 'Stoicism Today' blog as part of an ongoing commitment by the attendees to investigate matters further. In order to progress their investigations those involved organised a 'Stoic Week' to test the effects of 'living like a Stoic', inviting interested individuals to fill out questionnaires, follow a number of 'Stoic' exercises for a week and then to fill out another questionnaire to see if the process had improved their sense of wellbeing.

This process, by the nature of it, involved a limited number of Stoic ideas, ideas that mirrored many of the modern wellbeing and therapeutic practices.

Out of this original gathering (and the ongoing attempt at scientifically evaluating the 'effectiveness' of aspects of the Stoic training) grew the school now known as Modern Stoicism – a school that has distanced itself from Exeter University and has organised itself into a not-for-profit company so that it may disseminate its ideas through many mediums, including continuing the practice of promoting an annual 'Stoic Week' together with an annual conference called 'Stoicon'.

Over time, to date, other aspects of Stoic teachings have been added to the early 'live like a Stoic week' lessons, whereby such matters as moral standards are now included in the Modern Stoicism remit. However, while some may talk of spirituality, the teachings are kept neutral so as to avoid including the theism of classic Stoicism – as is expressed in the writings of Seneca, Epictetus and Marcus Aurelius.

Instead, there is a call for 'inclusivity' so as to ensure that the Modern Stoicism school is acceptable to atheists and the like. God is not part of Modern Stoicism. God is seen as a personal choice rather than as the fact of life that classic Stoicism saw God as.

Generally, Modern Stoicism is a cut-down version of the classic Stoicism, a version that ignores the pantheistic nature of classic Stoicism, almost totally rejects the foundation of the classic Stoic science and generally offers Stoicism as a therapeutic and intellectual exercise aimed at achieving 'happiness' and 'wellbeing' through the study of Stoic ethics in isolation from the physics and rationale that offer the understandings that lead to an understanding of the ethics.

From various on-line platforms it is clear that many followers of Modern Stoicism have not studied classic Stoicism, but rely on books written by proponents of the Modern Stoicism therapeutic ideas, such followers getting some level of comfort and understanding regards getting the life-problems they are trying to cope with into perspective.

Traditional Stoicism
This, at present, is a far less organised school, it being more an umbrella name for those who accept the theistic aspect of classic Stoicism. The

general intent is to try to be true to Zeno and the ancient Stoics and their beliefs in 'the one God' in that much in the classic teachings are centred in the belief in God as 'the universal governor and manager of all things.'

> *'There are two general principles in the universe, the active and the passive. That the passive is matter, an existence without any distinctive quality. That the active is the reason which exists in the passive, that is to say God. For that he being eternal, and existing throughout all matter, makes everything.'*
> Diogenes Laertius LXVIII.

The classic Stoic system, that Traditional Stoicism looks back to, offers an understanding of the nature of the Cosmos as being aligned with its view of God.

However, Seneca tells us:

> *'The truth will never be discovered if we rest contented with discoveries already made. Besides, he who follows another not only discovers nothing, but is not even investigating... Men who have made these discoveries before us are not our masters, but our guides. Truth lies open to all; it has not yet been monopolised. And there is plenty left of it even for posterity to discover.'*
> XXXII. On the futility of Learning Maxims

The person wishing to investigate the soundness of the classic Stoicism, and hence the authenticity of Traditional Stoicism, will look to as much information and writings as possible regards the foundations of Stoicism as initiated by Zeno and, in parallel to this, they will decide as to what is still sustainable in light of the advances in observational and experimental science to the modern day.

Opponents to looking back to the physics of classical Stoicism tend to try to ridicule some of the theorising of the ancient Stoics, theorising that was based on the then state of observational science. However, much of the classic Stoic science can be seen to be reflected in some of the modern scientific theories.

Which is why a member of the Traditional Stoic school will recognise that some of the ancient Stoic theories and ideas need to be improved on or rejected. But also will see that this is no reason to totally reject the whole of the Stoic physics – which includes a science that offers a sound explanation as to the nature of existence as an integrated whole and how we as individuals fit into that whole.

Those who investigate the classic Stoic approach to understanding life and how to live it and discover that the foundational principles are sound and in keeping with today's observational and experimental science and who then choose to make Stoicism their guide in life will be of the Traditional Stoic school, albeit that the detail of the beliefs and practice may be individualistic.

In doing so, the Traditional Stoic will be accepting of the foundational beliefs of Stoicism, which will start with the acceptance of the following as outlined by Diogenes Laertius:

'The Stoics divide reason according to philosophy (the love of wisdom) into three parts: and say that one part relates to natural philosophy, one to ethics, and one to logic. .....as some of them say, no one part is preferable to another, but they are all combined and united inseparably; and so they treat them all in combination.'

*'That the substance of all existing things is Primary Matter, ...
Now matter is that from which anything is produced. And it is
called by a twofold appellation, essence and matter; the one is
related to all things taken together, and the other to things in
particular and separate. The one which relates to all things
taken together, never becomes either greater or less; but the
one relating to things in particular, does become greater or
less, as the case may be.'*

*'There are two general principles in the universe, the active
and the passive. That the passive is matter, an existence
without any distinctive quality. That the active is the reason
which exists in the passive, that is to say God. For that he
being eternal, and existing throughout all matter, makes
everything.'*

*'To live according to virtue is the same thing as living
according to one's experience of those things which happen by
nature; .... Our individual natures are all parts of universal
nature, and that means corresponding to one's own nature
and to universal nature; doing none of those things which the
common law of mankind is in the habit of forbidding, and that
common law is identical with that right reason that pervades
everything, being the same with Jupiter [God], who is the
regulator and chief manager of all existing things.'*

*'The chief good is confessedly to live according to Nature;
which is to live according to virtue, for Nature [God] leads us
to this point.'*

24. A Stoic Prayer

Stoicism sees God as both the Logos and the Divine Fire. And, as Epictetus and others clearly tell us, the Stoic wishes to align their will with the will of God. The following prayer of acknowledgement follows in the path of these principles.

Mother-Father, I perceive thee as the Word of Being.
May I grow in wisdom and understanding,
That my thoughts, my words, and my deeds
Will ever become a greater reflection of thee.

Mother-Father, I perceive thee as the Flame of Being.
May I see your light ever more clearly,
That I may feel your warmth and your love
So that I may be at one with life and with thee.

Mother-Father, may my state of awareness ever improve,
That I will not lose sight of the true path,
The path of Good, the path of Inner Peace,
The path that is the Way of Harmony with thee.

Mother-Father, thee do I honour and trust.
As the only true guide,
The inspiration of being,
To thee do I surrender myself.

25. On Talking with the Cosmos

How does a Stoic approach the idea of talking with the Cosmos – and hence God?

From the Stoic perspective it makes perfect sense to recognise that we can commune with the Cosmos in that we share in its Logos – its mind faculty. Through the 'active principle' we are individuals while also being one with the Cosmos and all that is manifested within it. This aspect of our metaphysics offers a place for such matters as Socrates' daimonion, whereby we can be guided by a 'divine something'.

> 'We do not need to uplift our hands towards heaven… as if in this way our prayers were more likely to be heard. God is near you, he is with you, he is within you… A holy spirit indwells within us. One who marks our good deeds and our bad deeds, and is our guardian. Indeed, no man can be good without the help of God. … He it is that gives noble and upright counsel.'
> Seneca

This may seem contrary to Professor Murray's assertion that:

> Stoicism "was a philosophy inasmuch as it made no pretence to magical powers or supernatural knowledge."

But such is in keeping with the Stoic view of the nature of things. It is not magical in that it is not contrary to the Stoic worldview. It is not supernatural in that it is to be seen as being a consequence of the nature of the way the Cosmos is manifested.

Stoicism tells us that we can, in part, learn what God's purpose for us is and how we can best live by looking to the nature of the world that

God manifests about us and to the roles we are given in the play of life and by looking to the 'common perceptions' of humankind. However, Stoicism of old has also told us that there are processes whereby we can consult God for specific guidance through such things as the Oracle – something that the Stoic's of old studied and where they found there to be a statistical 'proof' that sound guidance was being given.

We are also told that the Stoics of old saw themselves as being on a par with 'the gods' while also seeing themselves as being a part of 'the one God', the God that manifests the Cosmos in a manner whereby the Cosmos is the body of God. By experience and by logic, Stoics see that at some level we can commune with God or some aspect of God (a daimonion or 'divine something' as described by Socrates) in that we share in the mind of God through the 'spark' of the 'active principle' that permeates our individual bodies.

Someone once asked me, why the God I commune with did not talk to them. I pointed out that, as the person was an atheist, it was not that God was not talking to him but rather that the person's beliefs were making him deaf and blind to God because of his determination to ignore anything that ran counter to his intellectualised rebuttal of all things that smack of religion.

To talk to God, it seems sensible that one needs to believe in God. After all, if you did not believe that you had a sibling, why would you try phoning that sibling? The same goes for communing with God, although God will 'talk' to a person even if they are not a believer.

Stoicism does a very good job of awakening a belief in God through the Stoic rationale that stems from the Stoic metaphysics that tells us that the Cosmos is being manifested moment by moment out of a 'prime material' that is permeated by the 'active principle' where the 'active principle' is akin to 'the Consciousness' of the modern sciences, and that is possessed of the same qualities that Stoicism attributes to God in that it is 'the universal governor and organiser of all things.'

When it comes to considering the nature of God directly, Stoicism offers 'the wisdom of the ages' seen as the 'common perceptions of humankind' that presents us with a common belief in a singular 'Something' that is responsible for the Cosmos being as it is, in that the 'Something' (the one God in Stoic terms) is 'the universal governor and organiser of all things.'

And just looking at the general populous it is to be seen, even if they claim not to be 'religious', that the vast majority of people have a passing belief in some form of God, in part as a result of a belief that our loved ones are always with us 'in spirit' - through re-merging with God, through passing on to some other 'domain', through reincarnation, etcetera.

(What happens to an individual after death is not an issue that was fully settled by the Stoics of old in that there is no 'common perception' within all cultures as to what happens – even though there is a common belief that what one has done in one's life is in some way and to some degree important when it comes to 'moving on'.)

In fact, most people have an innate belief in 'a friend beyond phenomena' and it is this belief that makes it easier to talk to the Cosmos. All we have to do to open the conversation is to talk to God as a friend, and then to be ready to hear an answer regardless of how the answer comes. That is, if an answer is necessary. Like any good friend, the Cosmos is always willing to just listen while we work out any answers for ourselves.

So how, today, does one approach the idea of talking with the Cosmos – and hence God?

Personally, when I talk to the Cosmos, I address it as 'Mother-Father' for I see it as our spiritual 'parent'.

Over the years I have found various techniques that are akin to the ancient Oracle (that is reported to have said that there were 'none wiser than Socrates') and other such ideas of old whereby we can receive guidance in a manner that bypasses the critical nature of our thought processes that might otherwise deafen us to direct communication. But an openness to communing directly with God is preferable to such 'party tricks.'

I will at times ask for help, guidance and/or encouragement, as appropriate, to see through some matter in life. And when some situation has come to fruition, I will ask what the Cosmos wants of me next by way of service to others and the common good.

Of course, in such communing, a good state of mind does help. While I have not been free of 'the slings and arrows' of life I have always been content with life in that I believe that the whole of life's events have purpose – even if sometimes the purpose is to be seen only in hindsight, if the purpose is to be seen at all. I accept that whatever happens, happens as it does because it is part of a bigger picture.

However, I also do not just rest on my laurels. I strive to try to play my part in hopefully determining for the better how things will happen as the flow of change that is Existence progresses. We Stoics are not just expected to 'accept', we are also expected to strive to cooperate with the Cosmos in determining how things will pan out for the better.

To do this Stoicism tells us that we need 'to make our will one with the will of God'. And we can better do this if we consciously consult with the Cosmos on what it wants of us?

The Stoic training involves contemplation on the nature of things and situations, especially by way of a daily self-applied 'de-briefing' regards how well one has stuck to one's Stoic life during the day. During such contemplation a sought for answer may present itself to an 'open mind'. But we also need to be open to receiving advice, guidance and even help from 'outside' of our own individualised state of being.

In talking to the Cosmos, I find it helps to have good intent. There is no hiding our inner thoughts and feelings from that which is actually, moment by moment, manifesting us as we are.

When it comes to asking the Cosmos for help, I have found that it helps not to overly desire a particular outcome, but to consciously confirm that I am willing to accept the outcome that actually happens - no matter what it is.

To accommodate this, sometimes I use simple methods such as suggesting to the Cosmos what it is that I have decided is the wise course to proceed along while at the same time asking the Cosmos to divert or block the course of actions I am going to initiate if such is inappropriate. Basically, I am asking the Cosmos for support to proceed with the particular course of action or to block it. This way I am seeking to ensure that I am not going against 'the will of God'.

Sometimes where action is called for but where my present course of action is not progressing as hoped for and nothing has come along to suggest that what is being aimed for is inappropriate, I have found that I will say to the Cosmos that as 'Plan A' appears to be stalled I am going to divert my attention to a 'Plan B'. However, I will let the Cosmos know that I am trying not to be impatient and will be content as to whichever plan comes to fruition – if either. For some reason that I have not yet fathomed, in letting go of any preference for the 'Plan A' I will find that being open to alternatives seems to free up whatever was holding back on the 'Plan A' and often the 'Plan A' will then move through to a successful completion. Possibly it is the Cosmos testing my ability to be accepting and patient or to see that I am not being overly attached to some hoped for outcome.

Another 'technique' I have developed is to 'make a deal' with the Cosmos – or more correctly, a commitment on my part. My part in such a 'deal' is to acknowledge and bring about what I need to do to prepare myself for the hoped-for outcome while setting myself a time period within which to accomplish what I need to do. I then ask the Cosmos to help nudge the necessary 'external' matters needed in the right direction as appropriate.

Sometimes when I am asking something of the Cosmos it may need time 'to get all of the ducks in a line'. At other times it is as if the Cosmos already had matters in hand and all that was needed was for me to ask – in which case there is an almost immediate response. One needs to be patient – God does not perform miracles; God only does what is possible. But with a nudge here and a nudge there, the flow of change can be guided to a position where one's prayers can be answered – if such is appropriate.

And of course, it has to be remembered that one needs to be careful as to what one asks of the Cosmos. The Cosmos may just give it to us in order to teach us a lesson. One also needs to avoid constantly pestering the Cosmos. There are times and places to consult the Cosmos, but generally the Cosmos has already given us all the answers we need, we just do not necessarily know the right question to ask. We have been given our life to live as free agents – not to be slaves to God.

As they say, 'God helps those who help themselves.' And that is not an invite to grab what you can for yourself – it may be better stated that 'God helps those who get on and do what they, with forethought, think is right.' That is, try to live life with good intent and, in all probability, matters will go as is appropriate. Not necessarily as one would wish, but as they ought to in light of 'the bigger picture' – the extent of which we are unlikely to be fully aware of. Hence, yet again, the need for acceptance.

So it is that while sometimes it may appear that the Cosmos is not answering our prayers, the lack of an answer is an answer in itself. It may be that all we need is the confidence to 'get on and do' to the best of our ability or it may be that we, ourselves, need to reconsider the course we are on as part of our own development.

Certainly, when it comes down to it, it is for each individual to approach the Cosmos as they see fit - but respect for the deity they are talking to and self-honesty will not go amiss.

There is however always one piece of advice that is to be found in the 'common perceptions' of humankind. Any guidance from God will always be to live a life of good. God never tells us to live a life of evil in that we are always encouraged to do 'none of those things which the common law of mankind is in the habit of forbidding' – especially unlawful killing. When we believe that we have had answers from the Cosmos we need to be sure that such is not a madness of a sick part of our own mind, as well as ensuring that we are not following the sick mind of some charismatic character selling us some perverse doctrine that is greatly at odds with the wisdom of the ages. God does not teach hatred.

26. On Telepathy and the Quiet Mind

How many people have 'felt' the anger of another person? Even without any visual signs, one can walk into a room and feel the 'atmosphere' created by an angry person. In truth, at all times, people are pumping out all of their feelings telepathically. They are creating telepathic fall-out.

We are all doing it, and we are all being subjected to the telepathic fall-out from everyone else. Of course, if the fall-out is that of contentment, pleasure or happiness we enjoy being subjected to it. The words 'All the world loves a lover' demonstrates this all too well. But when the emotions being transmitted are of anger, fear, frustration and such like, so it affects us adversely. Through telepathy we become empathic to the feelings of those around us.

Group hysteria and mob violence are extreme demonstrations of this. We start to have the same feelings and emotions as those we are being bombarded by. Normally our subconscious tends to filter out most of such unwanted fall-out so that it does not reach our conscious minds. However, if we are being bombarded with heightened emotions and feelings that we do not want to take on board, then we will probably find ourselves feeling the strain.

Nowadays many people are trying to 'open their minds' and such like. Often at the behest of some spiritual belief or fad. But all of the faiths of the past have told us to close down our minds. That is, not to have closed minds that are closed to new ideas and concepts. Rather that we should learn to quieten our minds on the telepathic wavelength.

We cannot stop our telepathic fall-out, but we can control it. We are advised that extremes of emotions are undesirable. Both for ourselves, but also for those around us. By training the emotions to follow the path of moderation we are avoiding being the equivalent of a telepathic ghetto-blaster. The ups and downs of our emotions can be disturbing for others who are subjected to our fall-out.

By understanding our emotions, we can learn to have stable emotions. This is the classic Stoic teaching that is so often misunderstood. The Stoics are often credited with guiding their followers to suppress all of their emotions, or at least with encouraging them not to show them. But this was not the teaching of the Stoas.

The person with calm emotions is not emotionless. The extremes are to have totally uncontrolled emotions constantly ruling one's life, or to totally suppress one's emotions. The path of moderation is to train the emotions to remain calm. The person who experiences calm emotions can appreciate the beauty of the emotions better than someone who allows theirs to run riot. The Stoics teach that the constancy of the calm emotion is what is important, as do many other schools of spiritual philosophy.

Such constancy ensures that others are washed with gentle waves of telepathic output, rather than being bombarded with 'loud' fall-out. Such constancy is the 'quiet mind'. And a quiet mind will better cope with the telepathic fall-out from others, as well as being 'open' to hear 'Another'.

'Without the Divine, there is no Stoicism'
– a published essay by Nigel Glassborow

First posted 15 Feb 2015 on the Stoicism Today blog at Exeter University.
Also published in 'Stoicism Today: Selected Writings II', edited by Patrick Usher of Exeter University, June 2016 on Amazon, ISBN 9781533463661.

Can Stoicism really be called Stoicism, without divinity? My aim in this piece is to show why you can't take the divine out of Stoicism. This is quite a challenge seeing as how the whole of the teachings are based on an understanding of the Divine Fire, or more correctly 'Phusis' – that is Nature seen as 'intelligent' and 'purposeful'. My apologies if I fall short of the task.

It cannot be enough to talk of virtue, striving for excellence and ethical theory. We need to see why we ought to choose the 'life of good' as is recommended by Stoicism together with all that implies. And the start of understanding not only why we should live the 'good life' but also the nature of the 'good life' is first of all an understanding as to how the Divine Fire manifests the whole Cosmos as the Oneness that it is.

Stoicism uses many words to describe and explain the many aspects of the living conscious Cosmos – however there is no separation between the Divine Fire, Phusis etcetera. The differing words are just human attempts to construct a framework of understanding – so if I shift between terminologies please follow Seneca's advice and see past the words in order to see the whole picture. Stoic teachings are not to be understood by examining the individual words or ideas in isolation.

While Stoicism encourages the individual to think for themselves, key to being a Stoic is acceptance of the guidance to 'Live in accord with Phusis'. The principle of the nature of the Divine Fire gives understanding as to Phusis being the intelligent and purposeful Whole of which we are a part – hence the idea that each individual is a 'spark of the Divine Fire'.

Any attempt at a 'therapeutic form' of Stoicism will fall short of the mark if it ignores Stoicism proper and only looks to limiting itself to the range of Stoic practices that are meant to be used as a means to train oneself to be able to 'habitualise' the Stoic life. The practices were never meant to be used as a standalone 'treatment', and there certainly is no such thing as Stoic Mindfulness, this being an adoption from Buddhism and other life philosophy systems. (Although maybe I am being a little pedantic about the use of the word 'mindfulness'. So as to avoid the connotations of Buddhist meditation and other such ideas that come with the modern use of the word, it is more accurate to talk of Stoic Attentiveness. Mindfulness has acquired connotations of looking into oneself, whereas, to my mind, attentiveness is more to do with looking outwards and seeing the bigger picture.) The thing is that the Stoic 'practices/exercises', without the rest of the teachings, are just CBT under a different title with all the limitations of CBT. It is known that CBT needs constant top-up sessions as its effects wane over time. (A search of the web will bring up many learned papers and articles to this effect.) This is because there is no 'teaching' as to one's place within the Whole behind the practices being taught.

Many attempts to 'restate' Stoicism end up watering it down, especially where teachings that are contrary to atheistic ideas are 're-interpreted' or omitted (presumably 'in the interest of inclusivity'). It has been said to me that 'people are free to incorporate theism into Stoicism if they wish to'. The Stoic pantheism that is the understanding of the Divine Fire is a teaching to be seen through all of the Stoas, so it is already incorporated into Stoicism. The Stoic theism where the Stoics of old recognised a 'god' is to be seen throughout the Classical writings – in fact part of what the Stoics of old were trying to do was to arrive at an understanding of man's relationship to the 'gods'. So it is not the case that 'people are free to incorporate theism' but rather that they are free to delude themselves by omitting it, which raises the question as to if they can then still call what they then follow Stoicism or call themselves Stoic if they reject the Divine Fire.

Stoicism is a life philosophy that combines knowledge and faith in order that we have a better understanding as to how to make the most of the life we have been given. It is 'the philosophy of the sphere'. The Stoics of old recognised the sphere as the shape achieved when all the inward and outward forces were in balance – and they state that the Stoic philosophy is just such a balance. All the key teachings of Stoicism are needed if it is to continue to be 'one of the loftiest and most sublime philosophies in the record of Western civilisation' (Encyclopaedia Britannica). And that includes the ideas about the 'Divine Fire'.

So down to business. Stoic 'science' is still valid in all of its key areas. Such was based on the 'common perceptions' of the day, logic and an element of faith. Compare this to today's quantum science which is based on 'imaginative' mathematical equations, instruction to rewrite the rules of logic and an element of faith.

Modern science is looking to try to understand the construction and evolution of the Cosmos. Stoicism looks to trying to understand how the Cosmos is manifested here and now. In years gone by the Stoics saw the Cosmos as being manifested out of an 'element' they called the Divine Fire. Bear in mind that what they called an 'element' we would today more likely call a 'property', 'quality' or 'state'.

To explain how the Cosmos is manifested it is seen that the Divine Fire had two indivisible aspects. There is the 'passive principle' that is matter without purpose – today this would more accurately be described as a sea of sub-atomic particles popping in and out of existence that are bashing around and not forming any of the elements or forces that are necessary for all that exists today to actually exist. In fact scientists are claiming that just such a state existed soon after the supposed 'Big Bang'.

In order to explain how anything is manifested out of this sea of chaos, the Stoics talk of the 'active principle' – this is what causes the 'passive principle' to organise and manifest itself as all the individualisations within the Cosmos. Scientists have glimpsed some of the workings of the 'active principle' and they call them the 'laws of nature' and 'the laws of science'. The scientists recognise the need for order, and in their descriptions of the quantum universe they are hard pushed to explain it without reference to what some of them call 'the consciousness'. The Stoics describe this 'consciousness' as the active principle – that is, 'the universal governor and organiser of all things'.

I would emphasise that the consciousness that permeates the whole of existence is not consciousness as we know it. It is used by Stoics and scientists to describe something akin to human consciousness, but beyond full explanation. It describes an essential aspect needed to explain how the Cosmos is manifested.

As we are part of this manifestation, as individualisations within the sea of subatomic particles, so we are part of the Whole. As the Stoics of old describe it, we are each a 'spark of the Divine Fire', or as scientists poetically describe it, we 'are made out of stardust'.

It is not a case of 'why you can't take the divinity out of Stoicism'; it is more a case of Stoicism being to some degree irrelevant, for we are 'sparks' of the living Cosmos whether we like it or not. It is just that the Stoics had recognised the fact two millennia before it began to dawn on the scientists that there has to be an immanent 'consciousness' that permeates the whole of existence in order to explain how everything fits together.

When the scientists eventually overcome their problems of marrying 'matter' and 'forces' with 'the consciousness' there might be less antagonism towards the teachings of Stoicism in this area. Some are ahead of the game. Sir James Jeans [11 September 1877 – 16 September 1946, an English physicist and astronomer] on talking about Quantum Theory stated 'The universe begins to look more like a great thought than a great machine.'

So we come to that little word that causes so much controversy – God. No, it is not a swear word as many seem to treat it. It is all a matter of definition, usage and baggage

As a result of the study of Quantum Theory, Martin Rees [Astronomer Royal] said: 'The universe could only come into existence if someone observed it.

No longer is it a case that 'believers' are allowed to have 'the God of the gaps in the knowledge of science' with the idea that even these gaps would be closed in time so eliminating God. It is now becoming apparent in scientific circles that God, the consciousness, is a prerequisite for a full understanding of all that is around us and for it to be made manifest. God does not just fit in the 'gaps'. God/Phusis/the Divine Fire/the consciousness permeates the whole of existence.

We Stoics, as the Stoics of old did, look to the 'common perceptions' and to personal experience. Throughout the ages there have been many differing attempts to describe 'the consciousness' that is involved in the manifestation of the Cosmos. Stoics look to this and see a common theme running through all such attempts.

In the Judaic/ Christian/Islamic traditions and many others there is talk of the One God. Other traditions talk of many gods and others talk of some form of 'state of being'.

We Stoics recognise that the Cosmos is a living conscious singular state. For want of a better word the English word 'God' is as good a word as any other to describe and recognise that Phusis, that is Nature as a living conscious purposeful entity, operates on a rather larger scale than we do. It also recognises that we ought to show it some respect. All of this is why we are advised to live in accord with Nature (Phusis, God, the Logos or whatever you want to call it).

By Stoic teachings, 'God' is immanent for the Divine Fire manifests us through the quantum world moment by moment and so permeates our very being. And knowing this, that we are 'sparks of the Divine Fire', gives us cause to study and take on board the Stoic teachings in order that we may better harmonise with the Whole.

However coming back to the issue of 'common perceptions', it is recognised that the Wisdom of the Ages (to be found as a common theme throughout most faiths) encourages us to live a life of good rather than a life of selfish self-interest. We are expected to even rise above the drive of 'the selfish gene' and to see the imperatives of the 'God', the Whole, as our imperatives – we are asked to live in accord with Nature 'so doing none of those things which the common law of mankind is in the habit of forbidding' while striving to fulfil our rolls in life to the best of our abilities.

Why? Because we are one with the Whole, so what harm we do to the whole we do to ourselves and what harm we do to ourselves we do to the whole. We may view in isolation what we see as our interests, but to do so is to bring about disharmony. We Stoics are taught that our interests have to harmonise with the interests of the Whole. Not just that of our family, our tribe, our society etcetera, but that of the whole

Cosmos at all of its levels. Stoics are taught to be selfish through selflessness. If it is in the interests of the Whole then it is in our interest. Even to the point that we must be prepared to sacrifice ourselves if necessary.

From the understanding of the Divine Fire comes the rest of the teachings to help the Stoic through the good times and the tough times. Stoicism will offer little help if it is treated as a coat that one can put on and take off as needed. Unlike CBT which aims to make a person 'feel better' about themselves at a particular time and place, Stoicism helps the Stoic all of the time to be as contented as possible with whatever is thrown at them for they will be looking to the bigger picture.

Stoicism is a philosophy for life (and death). It teaches an understanding of our place within the Whole. It teaches about human nature and ethics. It teaches us about our relationship to the One God, the manifestor and sustainer of existence. It then offers some practices/exercises so as to enable the habitualisation of the thought processes needed to enable the living of a contented life while also living an honourable life in harmony with the Whole.

So it is that the Divine Fire is the starting point for understanding all of the teachings. Until one understands the very foundation of the Stoic framework one cannot start to understand one's place in life. And it is through understanding one's place in life that a life of contentment (eudaimonia) can be achieved.